Shaping the **future**

The experiences of **blind and partially sighted** children and young people in the UK

RESEARCH REPORT 3

The educational experiences

of 16 to 25 year-old blind and partially sighted students

By Lee Smith, Sharon Da Cunha, Archie W N Roy, Issy Cole-Hamilton and Liz Clery with Sue Keil

Royal National Institute for the Blind

This report is the third of six on the RNIB survey, **Shaping the future**.
The series comprises:

Summary report

1 Research methodology and survey population

2 The educational experiences of 5 to 16 year-old blind and partially sighted children and young people

3 The educational experiences of blind and partially sighted children and young people aged 16 to 25

4 The social life and leisure activities of blind and partially sighted children and young people aged 5 to 25

5 The health and well being of blind and partially sighted children and young people aged 5 to 25

All reports in the series are published in print, braille, audio tape and on disk.
All orders and enquiries should be sent to RNIB Customer Services,
PO Box 173, Peterborough PE2 6WS, UK.

Tel: 0845 702 3153,
email: cservices@rnib.org.uk

COVER PICTURE: Figure by **Louise Simpson**, a blind student
at RNIB New College, Worcester

First published November 2001

ISBN 1-85878-479-4

Contents

Shaping the future research team

The Shaping the future research and reporting was undertaken by the following people.

The research

Group 1: Five to sixteen year-old blind and partially sighted pupils with additional complex needs

Kate Crofts (née Masters): Research design, fieldwork, initial analysis and reporting; further analysis and reporting by **Liz Clery** and **Issy Cole-Hamilton** with **Sue Keil**.

Group 2: Five to sixteen year-old blind and partially sighted pupils who access the curriculum within the expected range for their age

Anita Franklin: Research design, fieldwork, initial analysis and reporting; further analysis and reporting by **Sue Keil**.

Group 3: Sixteen to twenty-five year-old blind and partially sighted students

Lee Smith: Research design, fieldwork, initial analysis and reporting; further analysis and reporting by **Sharon Da Cunha, Sue Keil, Liz Clery** and **Issy Cole-Hamilton**.

Project administration: Angela Thompson with **Jessica Lubbock**

Project management: Issy Cole-Hamilton and **Louise Clunies-Ross**

This report: researched by **Lee Smith**; written by **Lee Smith, Sharon Da Cunha, Archie W N Roy, Issy Cole-Hamilton, Liz Clery** with **Sue Keil.**

Acknowledgements

RNIB would like to dedicate these reports to all the children, young people and parents who contributed in so many different ways to the **Shaping the future** project. We give them our warmest thanks.

We would like to thank the Specialist Coordinators in further and higher education, LEA Advisory Teachers, staff in a variety of special schools, RNIB Student Advisors and staff in RNIB regional offices and schools, without whose support and assistance this work would not have been possible.

Particular recognition must go to the original research team: Anita Franklin, Lee Smith, Kate Crofts (née Masters) and Angela Thompson.

For their invaluable advice and support, we would like to thank the members of the Advisory group: Marianna Buultjens, Anna Cannings, Nigel Charles, Joyce Chatterton, Fazilet Hadi, Liz Hills, Sue Holbrook, Annette Hope, Sue Johnson, Rita Kirkwood, Olga Miller, Kishor Patel, Pratima Patel, Stephen Porter, Pat Robertson, Richard Stowell and Professor Mike Tobin.

We are also grateful for the contributions of Dot Lawton and the Family Fund, Archie W N Roy for additional interpretation and contemporary commentary, Brenda Smith, Valerie Hibberd and Ann Boylan (RNIB), Ruth Sinclair (National Children's Bureau) and our editor, Hilary Todd.

November 2001

PART ONE

Introduction

CHAPTER ONE Key findings and recommendations

1.1 About the survey

During 1998 and 1999, RNIB asked over 1,000 blind and partially sighted 5 to 25 year-olds, or their parents, about their experiences, needs and aspirations. We also asked them to identify changes that could be made to improve the lives of blind or partially sighted children and young people generally. Responses from the youngest children and those who had communication difficulties/complex needs were made via their parents.

The agenda for the research was set largely by the young people and their parents. In 1998 more than 130 blind or partially sighted children and young people, or their parents, took part in focus groups to identify key areas of interest and concern. Questions for the main study were developed from issues raised by these groups, and covered a wide range including education, social life, independence and transport, health care and the future. The survey took place during the early part of 1999, by postal questionnaire or telephone interview.

Blind and partially sighted children and young people are not one homogeneous group. Although they all have the same basic rights, the services and support they require to realise those rights vary widely. Nevertheless some blind and partially sighted children and young people are likely to have things in common. With this in mind we approached the **Shaping the future** study as follows:

- Children and young people under 16 years old were grouped according to their learning ability. Those with complex additional needs affecting their learning ability comprised group 1. Those who accessed the curriculum within the expected range for their age formed group 2, and are described in the reports as "of around average learning ability".
- Group 3 comprised 16 to 25 year-olds of around average learning ability in full and part-time education. Group 4 comprised 16 to 25 year-olds who had complex additional needs.

Children of primary school age and those with complex additional needs were represented in the study by their parents. Those of around average learning ability aged 11 to 25 took part themselves. In this report (Research report 3) findings relating to young people of around average learning ability aged 16 to 25 years are in Chapters two to ten, Part 2, and research findings from those with additional complex needs between the same ages are in Chapters 11 to 14 in Part 3.

This research report, one of five detailed reports on the survey, describes the educational experiences of over 200 blind and partially sighted students who participated in the research through telephone interviews and 43 students with visual impairment and additional complex needs who took part with help from an intervener or their parents. These young people were drawn from all parts of the UK, from urban and rural areas, and from different types and sizes of family.

1.2 Functional vision within the survey population

Of the 425 children aged 5 to 16 of around average learning ability, just under one in five had little or no useful vision, three in five had severely reduced vision, and just over one in five, while requiring some support, had relatively good vision.

Among the 204 young people between the ages of 16 to 25 of average ability, just over two in five had little or no useful vision, just under two in five had severely reduced vision, and just under one in five had relatively good vision.

Of the 220 children and young people of all ages with complex additional needs, nearly three in five had little or no useful vision, and the remaining two in five had some useful vision. Among the 43 students aged 16 to 25 with complex additional needs, details indicated that one in three of these students had little or no useful vision, while two in three had vision that was considered useful or good.

It may be helpful for readers to understand what these degrees of sight impairment mean. Only a few blind people see nothing at all. Most have some perception of light, which may, for example, enable a young person to make out large shapes in a good light.

Young people with "severely reduced vision" in fact cover a wide spectrum depending on the eye condition they have: there are around 80 different eye conditions and it is possible for an individual to have more than one. Sight difficulties of this order, however, may mean that young people cannot use print as a means of learning and may find it difficult to understand and use their environment. Some can read large or even standard print but have severe problems getting around. Some cannot read print, but may be able to navigate their environment reasonably well.

Those whose vision is "relatively good" may nevertheless need support to read, often preferring large print, and they can be vulnerable in unfamiliar environments. Some young people need good light to make best use of the sight they have, while others function best in low light. The point is that every person with impaired sight is different and has unique needs.

In this part of the survey, young people of around average learning ability were allocated to one of six groups according to their level of functional vision. These are referred to in the report as "levels of vision", based on patterns of responses to a series of questions about visual functioning, detailed in Chapter two.

1.3 Education for blind and partially sighted students in the UK today

Current Government policy is to promote an "inclusive" education system wherever possible, in which blind and partially sighted students attend mainstream schools and colleges. Today, as there are few specialist colleges that provide for the needs of blind and partially sighted students, most are in mainstream placements. However, some blind or partially sighted students with additional special needs attend specialist colleges which may specialise in supporting students with specific impairments or with severe learning difficulties.

Most blind or partially sighted students require specialist tuition in the use of their residual vision (where appropriate) and/or in the use of compensatory strategies to develop other senses. They also need education in mobility, independence and daily living skills, as well as opportunities for personal, social and emotional development, specialist careers guidance and opportunities for vocational studies.

Over the last few years, provision and support systems have been improving slowly for blind and partially sighted 16 to 25 year-olds within education. So too has the degree of awareness on the part of educational establishments. At the same time, some provision has fallen short, and across the UK, it could still be considered patchy. Blind and partially sighted students have, to some extent, been aware of this: it can affect, for instance, what they choose to study, where they study and how willing they are to communicate their needs and assert their entitlement to an equal learning opportunity. This Shaping the future research report seeks to explore the nature, character and extent of current provision and clarify key issues. The survey evidence from 247 blind and partially sighted young people in further (FE) and higher education (HE) throws into stark relief how awareness of need and support to meet it can still be lacking.

Levels of disability awareness in general are currently still quite low across the UK college and university sector. It is only recently that the further and higher education funding councils have developed their guidance to the sector based on their own research activity. See, for instance, the growing awareness of disability and curriculum access issues on the part of the UK Quality Assurance Agency for Higher Education (1999), the Higher Education Funding Council for England (1999) and the Scottish Higher Education Funding Council (2000). However, it is likely to take many years for low vision and disability awareness in the college and university sector to rise to the point where their cultures are genuinely transformed and where equal access to provision for blind and partially sighted students can be assured. This report highlights the extent to which rhetoric about inclusive learning and widening participation still needs to become a reality.

It is also worth noting that the much needed Special Educational Needs and Disability Bill (Corlett, 2001) will bring this process further forward. It amends the Disability Discrimination Act (1995) to protect students with disabilities in sixth form, college and university. This legislation entitles them to an inclusive educational experience, making it illegal for students with disabilities to be placed at a "substantial disadvantage" because of their difficulties in accessing the curriculum and research facilities. By also placing "anticipatory duties" on providers, it puts disability firmly on the agenda for all further and higher education providers.

Funding is a crucial issue and mechanisms which support the additional costs incurred by blind and partially sighted students are currently administered by the Learning and Skills Council (formerly the Further Education Funding Council, FEFC) in England, Local Education Authorities (LEAs), the Student Awards Agency for Scotland and the Scottish Education Funding Council. In higher education, Disabled Students' Allowance (DSA) provides funding for personal readers and support workers as well as a specialist equipment allowance for the whole course. (See also Owen Hutchinson, Atkinson and Orpwood [1998] for a wider treatment of grants and benefits). In further education, blind and partially sighted students can benefit from additional units of funding applied for and administered by their respective colleges. A variable banding system of funding applies in England.

1.4 This research report

As students in the study were undertaking a wide range of courses, both academic and vocational, at various levels in schools, colleges and universities, their support and study needs were related to a variety of educational settings. We asked about the support they received to maximise their ability to engage in education – in terms of access to books and course handouts, access to the library, and the support received from staff and others. We also explored students' views about the social side of life at school, college or university, and the extent to which they felt included.

Some students responding to the survey had just completed their education and were moving on to seek employment; others were moving from one school or college to pursue their studies elsewhere. In responding to the questions, these students referred to their most recent educational experiences.

1.5 Key findings

The evidence from the survey shows that support in many mainstream colleges and universities must improve if inclusive provision is to meet the needs of all blind and partially sighted students.

The survey results show that while many students receive learning support and have their needs met in terms of accessible information, equipment and assistance, a considerable number do not receive all the support they need to pursue their studies.

Among students of average ability:

- more than seven in ten sixth form students were in mainstream education
- more than six in ten FE students were in mainstream education
- some students felt that their sight difficulties had affected their choice of

subject and course. Students in mainstream education were more likely to feel that their choice had been limited than those in specialist education

- while many students used more than one format, six in ten preferred large print
- under half of the students who said that large print was their preferred medium usually received it
- over one in four students had to wait for study and reference materials in their chosen format
- while three in five students had no problems, over one in five students found the college/university library difficult to use and a further one in five did not use it at all
- library records were not all accessible to visually impaired students
- almost six in ten students felt they took longer to do coursework than their friends
- one in ten students said they did not always get examination papers in their preferred format
- almost one student in five said they did not have access to all the equipment they needed, ranging from computers and associated adaptive technology to reading lamps. Cost was a major factor, information another
- while the majority of students felt supported, almost one in five higher education students felt they did not have someone to talk to if they had a problem
- more than one student in five relied on other people to take notes for them
- more than eight in ten students were generally satisfied with the careers advice received but a third of students had been told they could not do a job they had been interested in because of their sight difficulties
- only one in five students had been trained to find out about job vacancies though seven in ten had been taught to write CVs
- almost nine in ten students who stated a preferred occupation thought they would achieve their career goals
- when asked what needed to be improved, almost one in three students wanted better support in education while a similar proportion wanted to see changes in attitudes towards blind and partially sighted people.

Among the small sample of students with additional learning difficulties:

- parents were very satisfied with their child's educational placement, though fewer than half felt they had been offered a real choice in this
- several parents felt that the young people needed better access to materials in a format they could read
- some parents wanted the students to have more involvement with the local community.

1.6 RNIB recommendations

1.6.1 Inclusive education

In the drive towards an inclusive society, the Government and education providers must accept that inclusion is as much about the ethos and social life of colleges as it is about access to study materials and courses. RNIB recommends that:

- the Government should ensure that, as part of its inclusive education strategy, mainstream provision in further and higher education is adequately resourced to meet the needs of all students
- all educational establishments' policies, practice and procedures should show how they develop and monitor teaching and learning activities in which blind and partially sighted students are able to participate
- the built environment of the college, including teaching, learning, leisure and library areas, should always take account of the needs of blind and partially sighted students. Advice on refurbishment, redecoration and design features is available from RNIB.

1.6.2 Accessible information

Students should always be able to access study and assessment material in a format they can use. RNIB recommends that:

- all colleges and universities adopt and implement clear policies on making written information available to all students to those who are blind or partially sighted (RNIB provides advice and guidance on producing print, tape and braille.)

- the policies, practices and procedures of all colleges and universities should show how they facilitate the participation of blind and partially sighted students in the life of the college
- greater investment is made in access technology and its infrastructure to facilitate Information and Communication Technology (ICT) and internet use by blind and partially sighted students.

1.6.3 Attitudes and awareness

Blind and partially sighted young people say that attitudes towards disabled people must change fundamentally. RNIB recommends that:

- colleges and universities should set targets for staff training in disability equality and awareness, including awareness of their obligations under current disability legislation
- colleges and universities should ensure that all disabled young people know about, and fully understand, their rights under legislation, including their right to redress
- college and university careers services should do more to become informed about the capabilities of blind and partially sighted students and then promote employment opportunities, including vacation and part-time work, to these young people.

1.7 Conclusion

The Shaping the future surveys and focus groups provided us with unparalleled information about college life for blind and partially sighted students in the UK. It is the first study that elicits a significant quantity of its evidence from the young people themselves in such depth. This provides RNIB with a firm mandate for encouraging the continuation of current good practice in educational provision and working to achieve change where change is necessary.

References

Higher Education Funding Councils for England and Wales (1999). **Guidance on base-level provision for disabled students in higher education institutions.** HEFCE and HEFCW, Cambridge.

Owen Hutchinson J, Atkinson K and Orpwood J (1998). **Breaking down barriers: access to further and higher education for visually impaired students.** Stanley Thornes, Cheltenham.

RNIB (1999) See it Right guidelines. RNIB, London.

Scottish Higher Education Funding Council (2000). **Teachability: creating an accessible curriculum for students with disabilities.** The University of Strathclyde, Glasgow.

Quality Assurance Agency for Higher Education (1999). **Code of practice for the assurance of academic quality and standards in higher education: section 3 students with disabilities.** QAA, Gloucester.

Further information

Publications on housing and the built environment are available from RNIB. For details, call RNIB Helpline 0845 766 9999, or email cservices@rnib.org.uk for a copy of the RNIB publications catalogue.

PART TWO

Blind and partially sighted students of around average ability

CHAPTER TWO About the young people

This chapter provides background information about the demographic makeup of this group of students aged 16 to 25 and details of their eye condition and its functional effect.

2.1 Gender

- Sixty per cent of the student population in this sample were male and 40 per cent were female.

In all sections of the Shaping the future survey, a 60/40 split was found between males and females. The sample can also be compared with a gender analysis by Richardson and Roy (2001) of all self-declaring blind and partially sighted higher education students in the UK. In the academic year 1995/96, 1,944 students were recorded by their institutions as declaring themselves to be blind or partially sighted (UK Higher Education Statistics Agency, 1995/96). Analysis revealed that 58 per cent were male and 42 per cent female. The Shaping the future sample is consistent with this much larger student population, indicating that there are likely to be more blind and partially sighted young men than young women. Indeed, this is similar to the sample of 16 to 59 year-olds involved in an earlier RNIB survey (Bruce et al, 1991) with 43 per cent females and 57 per cent males.

2.2 Age distribution

This part of the Shaping the future research sought to obtain the views of those students who were in the post-compulsory stage of their education. Generally speaking, such students are aged 16 or over. However, within our survey sample, four students – three in school sixth forms and one attending an FE college – had yet to reach their sixteenth birthday. However, all fulfilled the research criteria in terms of educational placement. In terms of age, this group of participants was slightly skewed towards the younger end of the spectrum with half under the age of 19 and the other half aged 19 to 25.

2.2.1 Age and gender

There were differences in the gender distribution of the under 19 and 19 to 25 age groups. In the younger student group, there was an equal distribution between males and females (50 per cent were male and 50 per cent female).

In the older group, 72 per cent were male. For comparison, the Department for Education and Skills (DfES, formerly the DfEE, 1999) cites that, of all FE and HE students in the UK during 1998/99, 49 per cent were male and 51 per cent female. It appears from our research that fewer blind and partially sighted young women enter further and higher education and fewer continue in education past the age of 18 in comparison with their sighted counterparts. This may partly explain the numbers of males in our sample in both further and higher education and the relatively higher proportion of females in our sixth form schools and colleges. In other words, the balance of men and women in the RNIB sample, which was, after all, self-selecting, appears to be influenced by, among other things, the ages of the participants.

2.3 Ethnic origin

• Only 13 per cent of the sample came from ethnic minorities.

The number of students from ethnic minority groups was small, so that commenting on ethnic minorities as a group within the study was not possible. Overall, 26 participants (13 per cent) had selected an ethnic category other than "white" as shown in table 2.1.

Table 2.1 **Ethnic origin**

Ethnic origin	n	%
White	175	86.1
Pakistani	15	7.4
Indian	3	1.5
Black Caribbean	1	0.5
Irish	1	0.5
Bangladeshi	1	0.5
Other	7	3.5
Total	**203**	**100.0**

n=203

Nearly nine in ten students in the Shaping the future sample were white (86 per cent). The study **Staying On** (Keys et al, 1998) surveyed 1,432 students in FE college, sixth form college and school sixth forms and found that three quarters of the students were white (77 per cent), with the remainder coming from other ethnic groups, the largest of which was Asian. Both surveys found that approximately one in ten of the students were of Asian origin. Students from ethnic minority groups appear therefore to be slightly under-represented within the Shaping the future sample.

At home, most of the students spoke English although 15 (7 per cent) spoke another language:

- among these students, six spoke Urdu at home, four spoke Punjabi, one spoke Welsh, one Gujerati, and one Bangladeshi, while two did not specify the language used at home.

Thus for 93 per cent of the sample, English was their first language.

2.4 Visual impairment

2.4.1 Age of diagnosis

Nearly half the students in the sample had had their visual impairment diagnosed in their first year of life. In an older population, (Bruce et al, 1991) the proportion of those with early-onset of visual impairment was found to be lower (30 per cent), reflecting the larger proportion who become blind or partially sighted later in life. The RNIB survey of blind and partially sighted children and young people under the age of 16 (Walker et al, 1992) found that 80 per cent had had their eye condition from birth. This highlights the fact that younger groups are likely to contain more early-onset blind or partially sighted individuals.

2.4.2 Eye condition

- Nystagmus was the most common eye condition.
- One student in four said they had more than one eye condition.

Participants were asked to describe their eye condition in their own words. Two hundred and three participants provided this information, with one in four giving two eye conditions, one in ten giving three, and a few people naming four. If they were unsure about this, they were provided with a list of eye conditions.

Table 2.2 **Participants' eye conditions**

Eye conditions named	Number of times students named each eye condition
Nystagmus	34
Short sight (myopia)	28
Optic nerve atrophy	20
Albinism	19
Cataracts	19
Other: general comment on sight difficulty	14
Glaucoma	13
Astigmatism	11
Retinitis pigmentosa	10
Other: the back of the eye (behind the lens)	60
Other: the front of the eye (in front of the lens)	10
Other syndrome	6
Other: the whole of the eye	2
Other: visual pathways of the brain and visual cortex	2
Other: the seeing nerves	1

n=203

Note: one student in four said they had more than one eye condition.

Table 2.2 shows that the most frequently mentioned conditions related to the back of the eye (behind the lens), with almost three students in ten (n=60) falling into this category. Nystagmus was the most commonly mentioned specific eye condition, experienced by nearly two in ten of the students in our sample (n=34); optic nerve atrophy, albinism and cataracts were experienced by one in ten. Other conditions included myopia (short sightedness), glaucoma and retinitis pigmentosa.

2.4.3 Stable or degenerating eye condition

- 38 per cent of the group had experienced some change in their eye condition in the past two years, of whom seven in ten had deteriorating vision.

Making adjustments to deal with a changing eye condition and learning new ways of undertaking daily tasks is time consuming and can be very stressful. Sudden sight changes can have an adverse impact on students' work and wellbeing. They can be understandably fearful of further sight deterioration (Baus, 1999) and may have to come to terms with sight loss occurring over several years. This, in addition to adaptation to college or university life, places considerable strain on a blind or partially sighted student (Roy, 2001; Tuttle and Tuttle, 1996).

However, not all changes in eye condition are necessarily for the worse. Of 77 students (38 per cent) who said they had experienced changes in their vision, one in ten had experienced change for the better, while seven in ten had experienced deteriorating vision. Two students said that their eye condition fluctuated.

2.4.4 Levels of vision

- 42 per cent of the sample had very low vision, meaning that they either had no light perception or would find it difficult to see a friend's face close up.

Participants were asked what they were able to see so that their level of vision could be used as a criterion for subsequent analyses. Based on students' responses to these questions (detailed in table 2.3), we established three levels of residual vision, broken down into six sub-categories (see table 2.4). These sub-categories used in Shaping the future are similar to the five classifications described by Hyvarinen (1999) which are used for educational purposes, and which are also based on the young person's daily functioning as opposed to visual acuity alone. The levels described in this section give a practical indication of what students could see, that is, their level of functional vision, and differ from the criteria used to register people as blind or partially sighted.

Table 2.3 **Residual vision**

	See window in a room		Recognise a friend close to face		Recognise a friend across a room		Recognise a friend across a road		Read newspaper print	
	n	%	n	%	n	%	n	%	n	%
Yes	174	85	155	76	103	51	44	22	81	40
No	30	15	21	10	71	35	130	64	95	47
N/A	-	-	28	14	28	14	28	14	28	14
Total	**204***	**100**	**204**	**100**	**202**	**100**	**202**	**100**	**204**	**100**

n=204

The column headings in table 2.3 are taken from the questions put to participants about what they could see. The table shows that:

- the majority of students (85 per cent) were able to perceive where the window was in a room
- just over half (51 per cent) were able to recognise a friend across a room
- just over one in five (22 per cent) were able to recognise a friend across a road
- 30 students (15 per cent) said that they were unable to see where the window was in a room. This question was designed as a filter – if the student said they were unable to see the window, it was taken to mean that they had no light perception, and they were not asked any of the following questions. However, it appears from answers to subsequent questions about preferred media that some students may have misunderstood this question, and said they were unable to see the window because they could not see it clearly or could not see through it. It is likely that some of these students did have some light perception.
- 40 per cent of participants said that they could read newspaper print. This might include the use of a low vision aid, or close up nose-to-page reading – it does not necessarily mean that they could read it easily.

While these questions were subjective, they nonetheless give a useful indication of the levels of functional vision among students in our sample. The results have been used to group the students into three visual levels, according to how much they said they could see and these are given in table 2.4.

Table 2.4 **Levels of vision**

Levels of vision	Sub-categories: further descriptors provided by researchers	n	%	Total %
Very low vision	No light perception	30	15	42
	Can see light coming through a window, some can see a friend's face close to theirs	54	27	
Low vision	Poor distance vision – can not see standard print. Can see friend's face close to theirs and desks and chairs in a classroom. May not see a friend across a room, could not see across the road	32	16	39
	Low vision for reading print only – would need accessible media/equipment to read written material	6	3	
	Poor distance vision – can see close up but may find it hard to see across a room or road	40	20	
High vision	Said "yes" to all the questions about what they were able to see	37	19	19
Totals		**199**	**100**	**100**

n=199

Of the three levels of vision, the largest number of students in our sample fell into the "very low vision" category (42 per cent), closely followed by the "low vision" category with 39 per cent. Relatively few students in our sample had sight levels that placed them in the "high vision" category (19 per cent).

- **Very low vision:** 84 students (42 per cent) were in this group. Thirty of them were recorded as having no light perception, although not all of these students studied by non-visual means alone. It appears that some students could have misunderstood the question on light perception. The remaining 54 students could tell where the window was in a room, they could see the light coming through a window, some could see a friend's face when it was close to theirs but could not see a friend across a room, or the desks and tables in a classroom.

- **Low vision:** our sample contained 78 students who had "low vision". Thirty two of these students had poor distance vision and were also unable to read standard print, although they could see the light coming through a window, recognise a friend's face close to theirs, as well as see desks and chairs in a classroom. A further six students were able to function independently in terms of moving around the environment but needed visual aids/equipment in order to read standard print. Forty young people said that they had "poor distance vision" which meant that they could see to read newspaper print but had difficulty seeing across a road and in some cases across the room.

- **High vision:** 37 young people (19 per cent) were considered to have "high vision". They responded positively to all the questions about vision.

2.4.5 Preferred levels of light

Some eye conditions can result in sensitivity to light, while with others, bright light is useful. We asked students about their preferred levels of light for studying. The range of answers highlights the importance of asking students what works best for them.

Of 204 students:

- 47 per cent preferred bright light for studying
- 21 per cent had no preference between bright or dim lighting

- 18 per cent said the question was not applicable to them (this represented 36 students, 30 of whom said they had no light perception and six of whom had very low vision)
- 13 per cent said they preferred dim lighting
- one per cent preferred normal light conditions.

2.5 Other disabilities

- 21 per cent of students had other disabilities.

Of these, there were seven participants who had two other disabilities and one student who had three:

- seven per cent had a hearing disability
- seven per cent had a physical disability
- seven per cent had a medical condition.

Other conditions, experienced by only one or two students, included dyslexia, behavioural difficulties, speech problems and growth disorders.

References

Baus, S. (1999). **Commentary: psychological aspects of visual impairment.** British Journal of Visual Impairment, Huddersfield.

Bruce, I, McKennell, A and Walker, E (1991). **Blind and partially sighted adults in Britain: the RNIB survey – Volume 1**, HMSO, London.

UK Higher Education Statistics Agency (1999).

DfEE Statistics of Education – Education and Training Statistics for the United Kingdom 1999. **Post Compulsory Education and Training: Students and Starters** www.dfee.gov.uk/statistics.

Hyvarinen, L (1999). **Identification and assessment of low vision for educational purposes in developing countries.** Precision Vision: UK.

Keys, W, Maychell, K with Evans, C, Brooks, R, Lee, B and Pathak, S (1998). **Staying On. A study of young people's decisions about school sixth forms, sixth form colleges and colleges of further education.** NFER, Berkshire.

Richardson, J T E and Roy, A W N (2001). **The representation and attainment of students with a visual impairment in the United Kingdom.** Unpublished RNIB paper.

Roy, A W N (2001). **Student perspectives: discussions with visually impaired students on the effect of serious sight loss on themselves, their families, and friends.** RNIB, London.

Tuttle, DW and Tuttle, N (1996). **Self-esteem and adjusting with blindness.** Charles C Thomas, Springfield, Illinois.

Walker, E, Tobin, M and McKennell, W (1992). **Blind and partially sighted children in Britain: the RNIB survey – Volume 2**, HMSO, London.

Department of Education and Science (1981). **Education Act 1981.** HMSO, London.

CHAPTER THREE Educational placement

3.1 Placements

The students in our sample of 204 attended different forms of post-16 education.

Table 3.1 **Educational placement**

Current education status	n	%
School sixth form	20	10
Sixth form college	37	18
College of further education	70	35
College of higher education	12	6
University	64	31
Total	**203**	**100**

Seventy students in this part of the survey were at, or had just left, FE college – more than three in ten of the group. Almost as many (64), nearly three in ten were at university. Just under three in ten (57 students) were sixth formers, 20 of whom were in school sixth forms and 37 in sixth form colleges. Twelve students went to other, unspecified kinds of higher education establishments.

3.2 Placement groups used for the discussion and analysis

For ease of analysis, the survey findings are often explored separately for these three groups – sixth formers, FE college students and those in higher education – subsuming the smaller school sixth form and higher education college groups as appropriate.

Although school and college sixth forms are funded differently, the former coming under Local Education Authority (LEA) funding, and the latter under the Further Education Funding Council (now the Learning and Skills Council), the school and sixth form college student groups were combined in the survey. In terms of the educational experiences offered, there is a similarity in course content and course structures. In contrast, further education colleges offer a wide range of academic and vocational courses and take students from a number of different schools in the local area. Students in higher education pursue courses which are mainly academic in nature, with a national catchment.

Table 3.2 **Placement groups used for analysis of data**

Current education status	n	%
Sixth form	57	28.0
Further education	70	34.5
Higher education	76	37.5
Total	**203**	**100.0**

Using these new groupings, 76 students in the sample were at university or higher education colleges – almost four in ten (37 per cent). The FE college group was slightly smaller consisting of around three in ten students (34 per cent of the sample), and the smallest group, consisting of just under three in ten students (28 per cent of the sample) were in school or college sixth forms.

3.3 **Full-time/part-time courses**

Most of the students who took part in the survey were on full-time courses. Of the 57 students in sixth forms, all but two were studying full-time. The two part-time students were both at sixth form colleges studying for A levels/Scottish higher grades; one studying English literature and the social sciences and the other maths, music and physical education. Five of the 70 FE students were studying part-time. Three said their course was vocational and two indicated they were on other types of course, giving no further details.

Of 76 university/HE students, only two were studying part-time, both at higher education colleges. One was taking a post-graduate diploma in the social sciences, biology, maths and statistics and the other was studying diet/nutrition without specifying the expected qualification. The relatively low number of part-time students is similar to findings by Richardson and Roy (2001) who reported that blind and partially sighted students were far more likely to be studying full-time than students with no reported disability. This is hardly surprising since the Disabled Students Allowance (DSA) has until very recently been available only to students studying on a full-time basis.

3.4 Length of course

Thirty three out of 37 sixth-form college students were on two-year courses, three were taking one-year courses and one was on a three-year course. The question was not asked of school sixth formers.

Over half the FE students were on two-year courses, a third were taking one-year courses and six were on three-year courses.

Nearly five in ten of the university/higher education students in our sample were taking three-year courses while approximately three in ten were doing courses that lasted four years. Over one in ten were on two-year courses and a further one in ten were taking one-year courses.

3.5 Mainstream and specialist provision

- More than seven in ten sixth-form students were in mainstream education.
- More than six in ten FE college students were in mainstream.

Since the Warnock report (1978), the 1981 Education Act and subsequent legislation throughout the 1990s, there has been a steady shift towards the integration of students with special needs into mainstream schools and colleges, away from placements in separate specialist education. This research, carried out in 1998 and 1999, examined the experiences of students in both special and mainstream settings, at a time of considerable change when, increasingly, students were moving into inclusive settings.

We analysed the sample in terms of whether students were currently in mainstream or specialist placements. Higher education students were, of course, excluded from this analysis, leaving a group of 127 students.

Table 3.3 **Mainstream/specialist provision**

Type of provision	Sixth form school/college		FE college	
	n	%	n	%
Mainstream/resourced mainstream	43	75	43	61
Specialist provision for blind and partially sighted students	12	21	26	36
Other specialist provision	2	4	1	3
Total	**57**	**100**	**70**	**100**

n=127

More than seven in ten sixth formers and six in ten FE students were in mainstream placements, some of which were additionally resourced for students with visual impairment (namely, eight students in school sixth forms).

A larger proportion of the FE college group attended specialist establishments for blind and partially sighted students than the sixth form group – one in three FE students compared with one in five sixth form students.

3.6 **Educational placement by levels of vision**

• Students with very low vision were more likely to be in specialist provision.

Table 3.4 shows how students in sixth forms, FE colleges and universities were distributed across the three visual levels described in section 2.4.4. There was a similar distribution in the sixth form and university populations, but our FE college sample had a greater proportion of students with high vision.

Table 3.4 **Placement in sixth forms/colleges, FE and HE by levels of vision**

Levels of vision	Placement					
	Sixth form school/college		FE college		University/ HE college	
	n	%	n	%	n	%
Very low	25	44	25	38	34	45
Low	24	42	23	35	30	40
High	8	14	18	27	11	15
Total	**57**	**100**	**66**	**100**	**75**	**100**

n=198

Table 3.5 shows the type of educational placement (mainstream or specialist provision) by level of vision for students in schools, sixth forms and FE colleges. Although a slightly higher proportion of students with "very low vision" were in specialist establishments (four in ten), compared with those with "low vision" (three in ten), and "high vision" (fewer than two in ten), the number of students concerned is only small. It should also be noted that among the students with very low vision, a higher proportion were in mainstream than specialist placements (six in ten compared with four in ten).

Table 3.5 **Mainstream/specialist placement by level of vision**

Type of educational establishment	Vision level		
	Very low n=50	Low n=47	High n=26
Mainstream	30 (60%)	33 (70%)	22 (85%)
Specialist	20 (40%)	14 (30%)	4 (15%)

n= 123

3.7 Type of secondary school students had attended

- Similar proportions of the three student groups had attended mainstream schools – around four in ten.

Table 3.6 shows the type of secondary school students had attended with reference to their current educational placement.

Table 3.6 **Type of secondary school attended with reference to current placement**

Type of secondary school	Current placement					
	School sixth form/sixth form college		FE college		University/ HE college	
	n	%	n	%	n	%
Mainstream	23	40	31	44	34	45
Mainstream with resource base	22	39	19	27	12	15
Special school for blind and partially sighted pupils	4	7	15	22	19	25
Other type of special school	4	7	2	3	3	4
Both specialist and mainstream	4	7	3	4	8	11
Total	**57**	**100**	**70**	**100**	**76**	**100**

n=202

Examination of the three student sub-populations indicated that six in ten of those in higher education, seven in ten of those in FE, and eight in ten of the sixth formers had come through mainstream schools.

There were differences in the proportions of the sample who had attended resourced mainstream schools. While 35 per cent of the sixth form group had been to mainstream schools with a specialist resource base, 24 per cent of the FE college group had done so, and only 15 per cent of the higher education students. This may well reflect the recent growth in the number of resourced secondary schools with increasing inclusion, while time since leaving school and location within the country will both have influenced these findings at a time of rapid change in local authorities.

3.7.1 Attendance at more than one type of secondary school

Fifteen students (seven per cent) indicated that they had attended more than one type of secondary school. Moves between schools were explored to see whether level of specialist support might have had a bearing on each move. We found that, with one exception, students had moved to a school that offered more specialist support for blind and partially sighted students; also that four of the 18 students had experienced onset of visual impairment at secondary age. However, it is not possible from these data to be sure about reasons for a move of school – it could be for reasons quite unrelated to the student's visual impairment.

References

Richardson, J T E and Roy, A W N (2001). **The representation and attainment of students with a visual impairment in the United Kingdom.** Unpublished RNIB paper.

Warnock Report. House of Commons (1978). **Special educational needs. Report of the Committee of Inquiry into Education of Handicapped Children and Young People.** HMSO, London.

Department of Education and Science (1981). **Education Act 1981.** HMSO, London.

CHAPTER FOUR **Subjects and qualifications**

Students' choice of courses and subjects reflected not only their interest in certain areas of study but, in some cases, was clearly related to career aspirations or a desire to pursue academic work. Sight difficulties had also influenced the choices in some instances. In this chapter we examine the subject choices of sixth form, further education and higher education students.

4.1 **Sixth form students**

- Most sixth formers were studying two subjects.
- A levels were the most widely sought qualification.
- 81 per cent of students already had GCSEs or Standard grades.

Most sixth formers were studying two subjects (n=20), although four students were taking as many as eight subjects and another four were studying just one subject.

4.1.1 **Expected qualifications**

All the sixth form students expected to attain qualifications (or had just achieved them at the time of the survey) as shown in table 4.1. While roughly half of the sixth form school students were taking GCSEs and half A levels, a far larger proportion of students at sixth form colleges were taking A levels – around four out of five students. Some sixth form students were studying for more than one qualification, as the table below indicates – most commonly City & Guilds, RSA and a range of vocational qualifications.

Table 4.1 **Sixth form students' expected qualifications**

Type of qualification sought	Sixth form school n=20	Sixth form college n=37	Sixth form total n=57	
	n	n	n	%
GCSE	12	3	15	26
A level	10	29	39	68
AS level	1	1	2	4
Vocational qualifications	1	3	4	7
Other	1	-	1	2
Diploma (RSA, City & Guilds)	-	4	4	7

Note: a number of students were studying for more than one qualification.

4.1.2 **Qualifications gained**

Twelve of the sixth form students had previous qualifications, as did all but one of the 37 sixth form college students. Most students begin sixth form studies with some qualifications from their previous courses of study. Not surprisingly, most of the 57 sixth formers – 46 of them – had GCSEs, representing eight in ten of the students. A few had already gained an A level and some had a diploma or vocational qualification.

Table 4.2 **Sixth form students' previous qualifications**

Type of qualification	Sixth form school n=20	Sixth form college n=37	Sixth form total n=57	
	n	n	n	%
GCSE/ Standard grades	11	35	46	81
Diploma	2	6	8	14
A level	1	2	3	5
Vocational qualification	-	3	3	5
Other qualifications	2	4	6	11
None	8	1	9	16

n=57

4.2 **Further education college students**

- 91 per cent of the FE students already had some qualifications; 86 per cent of students had GCSEs.
- Half the students held or were studying for a vocational qualification.

4.2.1 **Qualifications gained**

Students in further education were asked whether they held any qualifications at the time of the survey. Sixty four of the 70 students said they had and only six had not.

Table 4.3 **Qualifications held by FE students prior to starting at FE college**

Type of qualification	n	%
GCSE/Standard grades	60	86
Diploma	9	13
Vocational qualifications	8	11
A level/Higher grades	4	6
AS levels	2	3
HND	1	1
Other qualifications	6	9
None	6	9

n=70

Of the 64 students with qualifications, 60 had GCSEs while nine students had diplomas, eight held vocational qualifications and six held A level, AS level or HND qualifications. Some students had more than one qualification.

4.2.2 Subjects studied

Around half of the 70 FE students (34) were studying one subject and most of the rest were studying two; however, one respondent reported that they were taking seven subjects. The most popular subjects were English and English literature (16), IT/computing (14) and business studies (14).

4.2.3 Qualifications expected

Half of the 68 students who were expecting qualifications were working towards or had achieved vocational qualifications, differing from the sixth form group, most of whom were working for GCSEs and A levels. Almost one student in three was working for A levels, Higher grades or HND, and fewer than one in six for a diploma (including RSA and City & Guilds).

Table 4.4 **Qualification expected**

Type of qualification	n	%
Vocational qualifications	34	49
Diploma (RSA, City & Guilds)	17	24
A levels/Higher grades	16	23
GCSE/Standard grades	8	11
AS level	4	6
Foundation	3	4
HND	2	3
Other	4	6
None	2	3

n=70

Note: twenty students were studying for more than one qualification.

4.3 Higher education students

- Seven in ten students were studying for a first degree.
- Over one in ten were studying for a masters degree or postgraduate diploma or vocational qualification.

4.3.1 Qualifications held on entry to higher education

Nearly all of the higher education (HE) students (75 out of 76) gave details of their qualifications at entry to their current university/HE course. Most students appeared to have followed a conventional path via GCSE or Standard grades and A level or Highers before entering higher education. One in five also held a vocational qualification in subjects such as computing and keyboarding.

Table 4.5 **Qualifications held by higher education students prior to current HE course**

Type of qualification	n	%
GCSE/Standard grades	75	99
A levels/Higher grades	57	75
Vocational qualifications	14	18
Diploma	11	14
Degree	4	5
Higher National Diploma	2	3
Masters degree	2	3
AS level	1	1
Other	5	6

n=75

4.3.2 Subjects studied and qualifications expected

More than seven in ten of the higher education students were working towards a first degree, more than one in ten for a higher national diploma (HND) and just under one in ten for a masters degree or postgraduate diploma. Three in four of the 76 higher education students in this sample were studying a single subject.

Table 4.6 **Qualifications sought at end of higher education course**

Type of qualification	n	%
Degree	55	73
Higher National Diploma	10	13
Masters degree	3	4
Postgraduate diploma	4	5
Vocational qualifications	3	4
Other	3	3

n=76

Note: two students were working towards two types of qualifications.

4.2 Did sight difficulties affect students' choice of subjects?

- A minority of students said that sight difficulties had affected their choice of subjects.

We were aware from our Shaping the future research with school pupils that some subjects pose more difficulties for blind and partially sighted students than others (Franklin et al, 2001). Secondary age pupils, for example, explained that they found geography, science and physical education more challenging – of 145 pupils, 61 per cent told us that their eye condition made geography more difficult, and of 162 pupils, 58 per cent said that their eye condition made science more difficult.

Our research found that the majority of students considered that their sight had not influenced their choice of subject or course. However, some of the post-16 students had tailored their choices to what they were able to achieve or believed they could achieve in further and higher education. For example, as these three students explained:

"I would have liked to have done the sciences but the experiments and close detailed work would have been too much."

Mainstream sixth form college student

"I deliberately didn't choose subjects that involved lots of intense reading, for example geography or history."

Mainstream sixth form college student

"Originally, I was studying information technology intermediate level, but I had to give it up at advanced level due to the graphics."

Mainstream FE college student

A total of 41 students answered our question about sight difficulties and choice of course. More than one in four of the 57 sixth form students said that their sight difficulties had affected their choice of subjects, as did one in five of the 76 higher education students and one in six of the 70 FE college students.

The 41 students who thought that their sight difficulties had affected their choice of course gave a number of reasons. These are shown in table 4.7.

Table 4.7 **How sight difficulties affected course choice**

Difficulties affecting course choice	n
Practical problems other than experiments e.g. woodwork or kitchen work	19
Problems with extensive reading or use of print materials	11
Chose courses leading to jobs where eyesight would not be an issue	5
Problems with experiments	3
Problems with close or detailed work	2
Chose option where had qualification or only thing good at	2
Need for refresher course	2
Choice of educational institution	2
Whether staff would accept them	1
Other	2

n=41

Note: some students gave more than one reason.

Table 4.7 shows that the most common sight-related factor influencing students' choice of course was the challenge presented by practical activities. This was cited by 22 of the 41 students who said that their sight had affected their course choice in some way. Eleven students mentioned factors such as their difficulties with sustained reading and extensive use of print materials which had influenced their choice of course. Five students said that they chose courses which would lead to jobs where their eyesight would not be an issue, indicating that some students begin to tailor their ambitions to what they think will be possible well before they finish their education. Problems with undertaking close detailed work were specifically mentioned by two students.

These are important findings and support other recent research by Simkiss, Garner and Dryden (1998) and Richardson and Roy (2001). In higher education, the distribution of blind and partially sighted students compared with sighted students is skewed well away from subjects such as architecture, maths, education and medicine, and towards other subjects including the physical sciences, computer science, social studies and humanities.

The participants in the Shaping the future sample suggest from their responses that blind and partially sighted students consciously avoid courses and subsequent potential career paths which they think will give rise to insurmountable barriers or a high level of stress related to access issues. This may also occur at an institutional level with students choosing to study at colleges and universities which have the necessary facilities (Hurst, 1996). What we cannot tell from our current research is how students in our sample had made their subject choices. Some may have lacked the right sort of career guidance and transition support and thereby limited themselves too much. Having said this though, blind and partially sighted students are now represented across all subjects of study in higher education within the UK. It is the frequency distributions by subject which vary widely when compared with all students.

4.4.1 Mainstream/specialist provision and sight levels

- Students in mainstream provision were more likely to feel that their sight difficulties had limited their choices.

A slightly higher proportion of students in mainstream placements felt that their choice of options was affected by their sight difficulties than students in specialist education. Of 85 mainstream students, one in five felt that their sight difficulties had affected their choice of options, while of 37 students who attended special establishments for blind and partially sighted students, one in six felt that their options had been affected by their sight difficulties.

A greater proportion of the students who had very low vision felt that their sight had affected course options. One in four of those with very low vision said this, compared with one in five low vision students, and only one in seven students categorised as having high vision.

References

Hurst, A (1996). **Equal opportunities and access: developments in policy and provision for disabled students 1990-1995.** In S. Wolfendale and J Corbett, (Eds), **Opening Doors: Learning Support in Higher Education.** Cassell, London.

Franklin, A, Keil, S, Crofts, K, and Cole-Hamilton, I (2001). **Shaping the future Research Report 2: The educational experiences of 5 to 16 year-old blind and partially sighted children and young people.** RNIB, London.

Simkiss, P, Garner, S and Dryden G (1998). **What next? The experience of transition: visually impaired students, their education and preparation for employment.** RNIB, London.

Richardson, J T E and Roy, A W N (2001). **The representation and attainment of students with a visual impairment in the United Kingdom.** Unpublished RNIB paper.

CHAPTER FIVE Access to information

5.1 The importance of accessible information

"If I can't read it, I can't learn it."

Visually impaired student.

Our questions in this section centred around students' preferred reading formats, whether or not these formats were provided, and how students fared when trying to use library services. It is hard to overstate the importance of this aspect of provision to students who, by definition, have real challenges in using standard print materials.

All partially sighted people and many of those who are registered blind will have vision suitable for reading print to some extent (Tobin, 1994). The extent to which people can read comfortably depends on their visual impairment and the amount of residual vision they have. Vision may be patchy, blurred, or the visual field may be restricted. Different solutions are needed for different conditions; for example, some people may need very large print, while others may prefer a clear, regular-sized font. (RNIB offers guidance on providing information in Clear Print as part of its See it Right guidelines.)

However, reading large print or using a closed-circuit television (CCTV) to enlarge material is much slower than reading is for people with average vision. Braille is also a slow medium to use. For example, an expert braille reader will read at an average speed of 90 to 115 words per minute (wpm) compared with 250 to 300 wpm for sighted readers (Rosa, Huertas and Simon 1994).

Because of the extra time needed to read information in any alternative format, blind and partially sighted students have to place greater demand on their short term memory, which may be more fatiguing. For this reason, it is important for blind and partially sighted students to be able to access materials in their preferred format and at the same time as sighted students.

Students' access to, and satisfaction with, available support will depend on the education provider's awareness of their needs, access to entitlements such as Disabled Students' Allowance (DSA) and additional college resources (RNIB factsheets 2001), as well as adequate assessment procedures. Overall provision and awareness in the post-16 sector has improved markedly in recent years (see for instance HEFCE, 1999; Green and Bartram, 1998; Green and Milbourne, 1998; Stefani and Simpson, 2000). The Tomlinson Report on inclusive learning (FEFC 1996) recommended that colleges of further education provide adequate funding for learning support for disabled students. However, a key factor continues to be the willingness and ability of blind and partially sighted students to exercise skills such as self-advocacy and assertiveness. Access to information does, to some extent, depend on a student making his or her needs quite clear (Wolffe, Thomas and Sacks, 2000).

5.2 Students' preferred reading formats

- 59 per cent of students in this sample favoured large print.
- Although smaller proportions of students used braille or tape, these were nevertheless the preferred formats for some.
- Many students used more than one format.

Students were asked which format they liked to receive their reading materials in, and if they liked more than one, to say which was their preferred reading medium. It is important to note that the questions asked about preferences – there is no guarantee that these were the formats students always or usually received. Many students listed more than one format.

Table 5.1 **Formats in which students liked to receive reading materials**

Formats used by students	Sixth form school/college n=57		Further education college n=76		Higher education n=70	
	n	%	n	%	n	%
Standard print	20	35	26	37	26	34
Large print	39	68	41	59	39	51
Braille	9	16	13	19	18	24
Tape	12	21	10	14	16	21
Computer disk	6	11	14	20	26	34
Other (e-mail)	–	–	–	–	2	3

n=203

Note: many students used more than one format.

- Large print was the most widely favoured format, with 59 per cent of students liking this medium. Although residual vision levels were similar among sixth form and university groups, (see table 3.4) a greater proportion of sixth form students said they liked large print.
- Standard print was the second most requested format, with some 35 per cent of students favouring this, many using low vision aids or other equipment to access standard print.
- Tape, braille and computer disk were all preferred formats nominated by some students. Braille was favoured by 24 per cent of university/HE students (where 45 per cent had low vision) compared with 19 per cent of FE college students (38 per cent of whom had low vision) and only 16 per cent of sixth form students (of whom 44 per cent had very low vision). However, another trend may be emerging. With advances in speech activated software, is it possible for students who might previously have learned braille to go through school without mastering it?

- 19 per cent of students favoured tape.
- Computer disk was favoured by 23 per cent of the whole student group, but by three in ten university students, compared with two in ten FE college students and only one in ten of the sixth formers.

Two university students mentioned the use of email in addition to other formats. Had this been included on our original list of options, it is possible that more students might have indicated that this was a method by which they received reading materials; the difference between email and use of computer disk is however likely to be minimal.

5.2.1 Favoured reading formats and levels of vision

Although many students used more than one format, they were asked to name their favourite or preferred format. Level of residual vision will clearly have an effect on students' preferences for a particular format. Table 5.2 shows the favourite formats of students whose vision was classified as very low, low and high.

Table 5.2 **Favoured format and levels of vision**

Students' favourite format	Students' levels of vision		
	Very low	Low	High
	n	n	n
Standard print	7	24	20
Large print	26	49	13
Braille	26	–	–
Tape	12	1	1
Computer disk	12	3	1
Other format	–	–	1
No preferences	1	–	1
Total	**84**	**78**	**37**

n=199

It can be seen that for the very low vision students, similar proportions (one in three) favoured braille or large print. It is likely that low vision aids were used to access large print. Unsurprisingly, tape and computer disk were preferred by more of the students with very low vision than by the other two groups. Just over half of the students with high vision said standard print was their favourite format (some may have used low vision aids), compared with three in ten of the low vision students and fewer than one in ten of the very low vision students (who were likely to be using standard print with readers or other assistance).

5.2.2 Use of other formats

Students did, of course, use formats other than their nominated favourite. Table 5.3 shows that students whose favourite format was a non-visual one (eg braille) frequently used other non visual methods, such as tape and disk. Large print users reported often using standard print or disk; the former can be read with a low vision aid and the latter read off the screen.

Table 5.3 **Other formats used in addition to students' favourite format**

Favoured format	Other formats used					
	Standard print	Large print	Braille	Tape	Disk	Email
Standard print n=53	n/a	10	-	-	4	-
Large print n=90	16	n/a	3	7	12	2
Braille n=26	-	1	n/a	11	9	-
Tape n=14	1	5	8	n/a	3	-
Disk n=17	-	10	2	5	n/a	-

n=200

5.3 Provision of books in alternative formats

- Fewer than half of the students who said that large print was their favourite format usually received it.
- Those who said that braille was their favourite format actually fared better – of 26 braille users, 23 usually received their preferred format.

Students illustrated some of their difficulties in obtaining materials in alternative formats:

"All the books were in standard print, so I had to take them to the CCTV or ask someone to read them for me."
School sixth form student

"We had trouble getting books into my medium of braille. Trouble getting around the library. The library did have a computer but it didn't have speech output."
School sixth form student

"No way I could read the books and no-one would read them to me."
College student

The evidence provided by students' responses to our questions shows that there are often difficulties associated with obtaining alternative format materials.

Following up points made by students in focus groups in the early stage of the research, we asked these students whether they usually obtained books in their preferred formats. Students who had left school were additionally asked about provision of books in their preferred format when they were at school. Details are given in table 5.4.

The table shows that while many of the students in our sample received study materials in their preferred formats, some did not. This was most evident in higher education, where nearly half the students were in this situation. Books are not readily available in alternative formats, but there are means of transcribing them and resources to assist with this. So it must be borne in mind that students in higher education had access to Disabled Students Allowance (DSA) and through this, to readers. The findings showed that:

- while over six in ten (65 per cent) sixth form school/college students reported that they usually obtained books in their preferred format, over three in ten (35 per cent) did not
- over seven in ten (71 per cent) FE college students said that they usually obtained books in their preferred format, while just under three in ten (29 per cent) did not

- almost five in ten of the higher education students stated that they usually had books in their preferred formats (49 per cent), and a similar number (49 per cent) did not. Two per cent said they were unsure about this
- among all the students, those who said that large print was their favourite format were least likely to receive it – only 41 out of 87 students usually received the large print they preferred. In the sixth form and FE college groups, students who did not routinely receive large print exceeded those who did
- those who said that braille was their favourite format fared better – of 26 braille users, 23 usually received their preferred format. Four out of five sixth form, seven out of eight FE college, and nine in ten higher education braillists usually received their preferred format materials.
- over half of those who preferred computer disk usually received it – 11 out of 17 students.

It is worth remembering when looking at these data that many students used more than one format, and did not rely entirely on receiving their favourite study format.

Table 5.4 **Whether students usually received books in their chosen format**

| Favourite medium | Usually received books in preferred format | | | | | | | |
| | Sixth form n=54 | | Further education n=69 | | Higher education n=69 | | All students n=192 | |
	Yes	No	Yes	No	Yes	No	Yes	No
Standard print	12	–	13	5	15	2	40	7
Large print	14	15	12	18	15	13	41	46
Braille	5	1	8	1	10	1	23	3
Tape	4	1	1	2	4	–	9	3
Disk	–	2	3	3	8	1	11	6
Other format	–	–	1	–	–	–	1	–
No preferences	–	–	2	–	–	–	2	–
Total number	**35**	**19**	**40**	**29**	**52**	**17**	**127**	**65**
Percentages	**65**	**35**	**58**	**42**	**75**	**25**	**66**	**34**

5.3.1 Getting preferred formats on time

- Over one in four students had to wait for materials in their chosen format.

Bearing in mind that reading alternative format materials takes longer and places a greater demand on short-term memory, it is particularly important for students who are blind or partially sighted to have access to materials at the same time as other students. Although 72 per cent of students surveyed said they did not have to wait for alternative formats, 28 per cent did, nearly half of whom used large print.

Table 5.5 **Students who said that they had to wait for preferred format books**

| Favourite medium | Had to wait for preferred format books | | | | | | | |
| | Sixth form n=36 | | Further education n=38 | | Higher education n=53 | | All n=127 | |
	Yes	No	Yes	No	Yes	No	Yes	No
Standard print	3	9	2	11	1	15	6	35
Large print	9	6	4	6	4	11	17	23
Braille	1	4	1	7	2	8	4	19
Tape	1	3	1	-	1	3	3	6
Disk	-	-	-	3	4	4	4	7
Other format	-	-	-	1	-	-	-	1
No preferences	-	-	2	-	-	-	2	-
Totals	**14**	**22**	**10**	**28**	**12**	**41**	**36**	**91**

As table 5.5 shows, a greater proportion of those students who favoured the use of large print indicated that they had to wait for this compared with other formats.

Although it is possible to produce materials relatively easily in large print using photocopiers and word processors, there is the issue of copyright to address. A larger proportion of very low vision students were in specialist education where braille resources are more plentiful and ordering systems often better established.

Numbers of students using tape and disk were low, but approximately half of these students said that they had to wait for materials in these formats.

It is notable that one in six students using standard print also had to wait for some books, so findings for visually impaired students must be interpreted in this context. Certain reference books are likely to be in demand on any course of study, particularly at times when reference is made by lecturers to specific topics or authors.

Table 5.6 **Students who usually received preferred format handouts**

| Favourite medium | Usually received handouts in preferred format | | | | | | | |
| | Sixth form students n=55 | | Further education n=69 | | Higher education n=73 | | All students n=197 | |
	Yes	No	Yes	No	Yes	No	Yes	No
Standard print	12	-	18	1	17	4	47	5
Large print	23	7	27	3	21	7	71	17
Braille	4	2	8	1	6	5	18	8
Tape	5	-	2	1	2	2	9	3
Disk	1	1	5	-	6	3	12	4
Other format	-	-	1	-	-	-	1	-
No preferences	-	-	2	-	-	-	2	-
Totals	**45**	**10**	**63**	**6**	**52**	**21**	**160**	**37**

n=197

5.3.2 Provision of handouts in alternative formats

• Four in five students usually received handouts in their preferred medium.

Students were also asked whether they usually received handouts in their preferred formats:

Table 5.6 shows that of 197 students who answered the question about handouts, 81 per cent said they usually received them in their preferred formats, while 19 per cent did not. Additionally:

- higher education students were least likely to receive materials in their preferred format. Seven in ten higher education students received materials in their preferred format, compared with eight in ten sixth formers and nine in ten further education students
- braillists were slightly less likely than large print users to say they usually received preferred format handouts. Eight in ten large print readers were usually given their preferred format handouts, as were seven in ten braillists
- the number of tape and disk users was low, 12 and 16 respectively. Three in four of these students were usually given preferred format materials.

Overall out of 160 students who responded, 21 per cent said that they had to wait for handouts in their preferred format:

- higher education students were more likely to have to wait than those in other establishments. Three in ten higher education students had to wait compared with two in ten sixth form and FE college students
- large print and braille users were equally likely to have to wait for handouts. Three in ten students said they had to wait for these formats
- numbers of tape and disk users were small, but approximately three in ten tape users and two in ten disk users reported having to wait for handouts in these preferred formats.

5.3.3 Provision of materials in preferred formats with reference to placement

- Nine in ten students in special schools/colleges for blind and partially sighted students were usually given access to books in their preferred formats.
- Six in ten students in mainstream provision were usually given access to books in their preferred formats.

We expected to find that students' placement in mainstream or specialist provision would affect access to books and handouts in alternative formats. The hypothesis that specialist schools and colleges would be better able to meet needs is borne out by students' experiences.

With regard to books:

- of 37 students who attended specialist schools and colleges for blind and partially sighted students, nine in ten were usually provided with books in their preferred format (one did not respond). None of the students who went to other types of specialist schools said that they usually received preferred format books
- of 32 students who attended specialist establishments for blind and partially sighted students, only two in ten said they had had to wait for books in their preferred format
- of 83 students who went to mainstream establishments, six in ten were usually provided with preferred format books (one did not respond)
- of 56 mainstream students who answered this question, six in ten said that they had had to wait for preferred format books. One in ten put "not applicable".

The provision of handouts showed a similar pattern:

- all 38 students who attended specialist schools and colleges for blind and partially sighted students usually received handouts in their preferred formats
- only one of the 38 students who attended a specialist establishment for blind and partially sighted students said they had had to wait for preferred format handouts. One student was not sure. None of the three students who attended other types of specialist establishments said they usually received preferred format handouts
- while more than eight in ten of the 83 mainstream students were usually given handouts in their preferred formats, almost two in ten were not
- of 72 mainstream students who answered the question, over seven in ten usually received handouts in their preferred format and two in ten said they had to wait for these. Fewer than one in ten students said they were not sure or this was "not applicable".

Overall, 21 per cent of students who responded to the question said that they had to wait for handouts in their preferred format. Over half of these students were large print users.

5.4 Using library services at school, college or university

Many students reported considerable difficulty with using the library at school, college or university. Several factors contributed to their difficulties:

- materials not being available in their preferred format:

  "All the books were in print. Someone had to either read them to me or translate them into braille."

  Mainstream sixth form student

- difficulty with reading signs and labels:

  "Because I couldn't read the signs on the wall, I couldn't read which book was which, and once I'd found the book, it was very difficult to see the page I wanted. It takes a very long time to find anything".

  Student's comments on both school and college

  "I find it difficult to look for books on the shelf. I cannot see the reference number or titles."

  University student

- poor lighting:

  "Due to the low level of lighting, titles of books were difficult to discern."

  University student

- inaccessible computer equipment for finding books:

  "All the information is on the computer which doesn't have speech."

  University student

  "Inadequate computer software for accessibility for disabled people. No screen enlargers. No large screens."

  University student

- busy or sometimes unhelpful staff:

  "I would always have to take someone with me generally because the assistance at the library was not always useful. You had to know exactly what you wanted to get any assistance."

  University student

"**Librarians didn't seem to care, did not help me….**"

Higher education college student

"**Everyone who could help is busy.**"

University student

However, many students responded that staff went out of their way to help as this statement illustrates:

"**…the assistants are very very helpful and they go up the stairs no matter how many times you ask.**"

Higher education college student

5.4.1 Use of the library: all students

- More than one in five students found the school, college or university library difficult to use and a further one in five did not use it at all.

Using the library is an important part of learning, particularly for higher education students for whom success on courses requires the ability to learn and research independently.

Table 5.7 **Ease of use of the library**

Ease of use of the library	Placement							
	Sixth form		Further education		Higher education		Total	
	n=57		n=70		n=75		n=202	
	n	%	n	%	n	%	n	%
Easy	16	28	30	43	13	17	59	29
OK	18	32	16	23	24	32	58	29
Difficult	8	14	8	11	29	39	45	22
Not used	15	26	16	23	9	12	40	20
Total	**57**	**100**	**70**	**100**	**75**	**100**	**202**	**100**

n=202

- Fewer than two in ten higher education students found the library easy to use, compared with almost three in ten sixth form and four in ten FE students.
- Students in higher education were the most likely group to report finding using the library difficult: almost four in ten higher education students said this compared with approximately one in ten FE college and sixth form students.
- Despite the difficulty higher education students reported in using the library, just over one in ten had not used the library, compared with more than two in ten FE college students, and nearly three in ten sixth form students. As indicated earlier, this is likely to reflect the importance of library use in higher education, and also the fact that college and university libraries do not routinely stock materials in alternative media.

Various factors in addition to educational placement are likely to impact on library use, such as visual levels and preferred media. These are explored below.

5.4.2 Library use and mainstream/specialist education

Library use was explored with reference to the placement of sixth form and FE students.

Table 5.8 **Mainstream/specialist placement and library use among sixth form and FE students**

Ease of use of the library	Type of placement			
	Mainstream education	Specialist for blind and partially sighted students	Other special education	Total
Easy	33	13	–	46
OK	24	9	1	34
Difficult	13	2	1	16
Not used	16	14	1	31
Total	**86**	**38**	**3**	**127**

n=127

The table indicates that students may be less likely to use the library if they attend a specialist school or college. While two in ten mainstream students had not used their library, nearly four in ten specialist students reported that they had not used their school or FE college library.

Of those who used the library, only one in 20 specialist students said they found the library difficult to use, compared with three in 20 mainstream students.

5.4.3 Use of the library and levels of vision

As could be expected, students' levels of vision affected their experience of using the library. For a description of the three categories of levels of vision, see section 2.4.4.

Table 5.9 **Use of the library by levels of vision: all students**

Ease of use of the library	Level of vision			
	Very low	Low	High	Total
Easy	13	25	19	57
OK	23	25	9	57
Difficult	20	19	4	43
Not used	28	8	4	40
Total	**84**	**77**	**36**	**197**

n=197

- Students with very low vision were least likely to have used the library. One in three students with very low vision said they had not used the library, compared with one in ten of the students with low vision and high vision.
- The data show that while just over one in two of the students with high vision reported finding the library easy to use, one in three of the low vision students and only approximately one in seven with very low vision agreed with this.
- Likewise, students were more likely to find the library difficult to use if they had less vision. One in four students with very low and low vision found the library difficult to use, while only one in ten of the students with high vision did so.

5.4.4 Difficulties in using the library

Those who said they found using the library difficult were asked to indicate why this was so. All the students gave similar reasons wherever they were being educated. Forty five students reported 91 reasons for their difficulties in using the library, nearly two thirds of which came from students in higher education.

Table 5.10 Difficulties in using the library at school, college or university: all students

Reasons for difficulties using the library	Number of responses
Getting around library or access to books	19
Difficult to find books due to small print on covers	15
Getting books in appropriate format	13
Problems with computers	11
Poor selection of books	6
Librarian no time or unwilling to assist	5
No need to use library	5
Difficult to find books due to small writing on index cards	3
Rely on other people's help	3
Difficult to read signs or instructions	3
Difficult to find books due to poor or illogical layout	3
Poor lighting	2
Other eg. buy books myself or get them elsewhere	3
Total	**91**

n=45 students

Getting around the library and accessing the books was the most common difficulty students experienced: two in five of the students who had found using the library difficult gave this as a reason. Small print on book spines and covers did not help and caused difficulties for one in three who reported difficulties. One in five students mentioned problems getting hold of books in their preferred format. One in five mentioned problems with computers – nine of these eleven were in higher education, for whom accessing books would be made considerably easier if the computers were suitably adapted to enable them to locate the items they wanted. Possibly linked to this, four of the five students who said the librarians were too busy or unwilling to assist were in higher education. Other difficulties students mentioned included small writing on index cards, problems reading signs or instructions, a poor selection of books, and difficulties finding books because of poor or apparently illogical library layout.

References

Green, M and Bartram, D (1998). **Initial assessment to identify learning needs.** Further Education Development Agency.

Green, M and Milbourne, L (1998). **Making learning support work.** Further Education Development Agency.

Higher Education Funding Councils for England and Wales (1999). **Guidance on base-level provision for disabled students in higher education institutions.** Cambridge HEFCE and HEFCW.

RNIB (1999) See it Right guidelines. RNIB, London.

RNIB Student Factsheet (2001). Financial assistance for blind and partially sighted students. RNIB, London.

Rosa, A, Huertas, and Simon, C and HUERTAS JA (1994) cited in Simon and Heurtas, JA (1998). **How Blind Readers Perceive and Gather Information Written in Braille.** Journal of Visual Impairment and Blindness May.
AFB Press, New York.

Stefani, L and Simpson, A (2000). **Creating an Accessible curriculum – the challenge for higher education.** The Skill Journal, 68, Skill: National Bureau for Students with Disabilities, London.

Tobin, M (1994). **Assessing Visually Handicapped People - An Introduction to Test Procedure.** David Fulton Publishers, London.

Tomlinson Report Further Education Funding Council Learning Difficulties and/or Disabilities Committee (1996). **Inclusive Learning.** (Chairman, John Tomlinson.) FEFC, Coventry.

Wolffe, K E, Thomas, L K and Sacks, SZ (2000). **Focused on: Social skills for teens and young adults with visual impairments.** American Foundation for the Blind, New York.

CHAPTER SIX Dealing with coursework and examinations

We were interested to know how blind and partially sighted students managed their coursework and examinations. For example, how did they take notes? Did they find that coursework took them longer than their sighted friends? Did they get their examination papers in their preferred media and on time? This chapter explores these aspects of students' lives.

6.1 Homework, coursework and revision

- Almost six in ten students felt they took longer to do coursework than their sighted friends.

Students were asked about the time they spent doing coursework or home study compared with their friends, and whether homework or exam revision caused them eyestrain. 58 per cent of students said that they believed coursework took them longer, while 61 per cent reported that they often got eyestrain as a result of doing coursework.

".... The first four months were hell as I couldn't see and didn't have enough time to do my work."
Student at FE college aged 18

Reading by sighted as well as by non-sighted methods takes longer for blind and partially sighted students as explained in Chapter five. Adaptive technology can also break down, causing delays and associated frustration. In addition though, blind and partially sighted students strive to succeed on a par with other students (Richardson and Roy, 2001; Roy, 2001) and their levels of attainment are very similar when compared with other students. They often choose to pay a price in time spent; all the more reason to ensure that blind and partially sighted students are supported adequately, that their college staff are trained in low vision awareness, and that students know how to manage their time effectively.

6.1.2 Homework and coursework by levels of vision

When the questions on studying are explored by levels of vision, it is clear that this has an effect on students' speed of working and/or eyestrain.

- 58 per cent of the 199 students who answered this question said coursework took them longer than their friends. Of this group of 116 students, 48 per cent had very low vision, 40 per cent had low vision, and 12 per cent had high vision. This underlines the fact that blind and partially sighted students with a severe visual impairment need additional time to work with all types of written, printed or brailled material.

- We found that of 120 students who said that they often got eyestrain when doing their coursework, 36 per cent had very low vision, 46 per cent had low vision, and 18 per cent had high vision.

- A similar pattern was found for the question about eyestrain and examinations. Forty seven per cent of students with low vision said they often experienced eyestrain when revising for exams compared with 35 per cent of very low vision students and 18 per cent of high vision students. Sixteen per cent of very low vision students put "not applicable" for this question, in most cases because they used non-visual methods for revision.

- Of 199 students, 15 per cent (30) said that they did not have the equipment needed at home to do their coursework and studying. Half of these students had very low vision (15), and of the other half, ten had low vision and five had high vision. This suggests that students with very low vision were least likely to have the equipment they needed at home, although the reasons for this were not explored.

6.2 Taking notes

When students were asked how they usually made notes during lectures, several reported using different methods as appropriate or convenient, as shown in table 6.1. More than two in five students (43 per cent) said that notes were prepared by their teacher or lecturer. In view of the comments from some students it would appear that this is not always straightforward:

"I have to nag to get handouts. They never seem to know about my difficulties."

University student aged 18

"There are a lot of handouts. I don't get the benefit of these handouts. I only get a summary…"

Student at higher education college aged 21

"I could use someone to read to me more and have more braille books and to have my handouts given out to me quicker so I can keep up with the other students."

University student aged 20

Table 6.1 **Methods students used to take notes**

Note-taking method	Sixth form n=57		Further education n=70		Higher education n=77		All students n=204	
	n	%	n	%	n	%	n	%
Take them myself	37	65	37	53	33	43	107	53
Teacher/lecturer prepares notes eg photocopies	31	54	28	40	28	36	87	43
Computer/laptop/ computer with speech	17	30	19	27	17	22	53	26
Tape recorder/ dictaphone	6	11	11	16	28	36	45	22
Electronic brailler/ Perkins brailler	6	11	10	14	3	4	19	9
Friends take notes, type up, borrow, photocopy notes	6	11	3	4	13	17	22	11
Supply teacher/ classroom assistant takes notes	4	7	4	6	5	6	13	6
Rely on memory, write notes later	2	4	4	6	4	5	10	5
Other methods	4	7	1	1	2	3	7	3
Reader takes notes and types them up	-	-	3	4	12	16	15	7
Someone else takes notes, and types them up	3	5	3	4	1	1	7	3

n=204

In each group, the largest proportion of students took their own notes: over six in ten of the sixth formers, five in ten of those at FE college and four in ten of the higher education students. The second most common method was to use handouts from teachers or lecturers; sixth form students were most likely to get these: 54 per cent compared with 40 per cent of FE and 36 per cent of higher education students. The third most widely used note–taking method for sixth form and FE college students was using computers; 30 per cent of sixth form students and 27 per cent of FE college students used computers to take notes. This was less common for the higher education students, 22 per cent of whom made their notes on computers.

"Notes for lectures are a problem as I have to write them down then type them into a format I can work from at home."

University student aged 20

For higher education students, the third most common note-taking method was a tape recorder or dictaphone, used by 36 per cent, while in contrast, only 11 per cent of sixth formers and 16 per cent of FE students used this method. This might be due to the volume of notes taken in higher education. It is also slightly alarming. Almost all the higher education students were full-time and often each hour's recording would generate more than one additional hour's work in replaying, selection of relevant material from the tape, and so on. In instances where students did not select relevant lecture material during the recording, it may often be the case that additional note-taking strategies were desirable but lacking.

The type of educational establishment had some bearing on note-taking methods. Higher education students made the most use of readers – 16 per cent of higher education students used readers compared with three per cent of FE students and none of the sixth form group; this is likely to be due to the availability of the Disabled Students Allowance to those in higher education.

6.2.1 Differences in note-taking methods between secondary, further and higher education

One hundred and three college and university students said that they were taking notes differently now compared with when they were at secondary school. The question was put to sixth form college, FE and higher education students. Of 107 sixth form college and FE students, nearly half – 48 per cent (51) – said they used different methods now compared with when they were at school. Of 77 higher education students, nearly seven in ten (52) said they used different note-taking methods compared with what they had used at secondary school. Specific differences are given as percentages below:

- 38 per cent of higher education students and 43 per cent of the sixth form and FE college students cited taking their own notes as a method they had used at school, but did not use now
- 31 per cent of higher education students and 20 per cent of sixth form and FE college students reported using a computer/laptop or computer with speech at school, but not now
- 17 per cent of higher education students and 16 per cent of sixth form college and FE college students reported that they no longer received handouts and notes as they had done from teachers at school
- 23 per cent of higher education students and 14 per cent of sixth form or FE college students reported using a braille machine at school, which they no longer used.

6.2.2 Note taking and levels of vision

- Students with lower levels of vision were most likely to use technology to take notes.
- A high proportion of students depended on someone else to take notes for them.

We expected to find that students' levels of vision would be related to note-taking methods. As students tended to use more than one note-taking method, (probably dependent on the task), the total number of responses given in table 6.2 exceeds the number of students.

Table 6.2 **Note-taking methods and levels of vision**

Method of taking notes	Visual level			Total responses	
	Very low n=84	Low n=78	High n=37	n=199	
	n	n	n	n	%
Take them myself	23	52	29	104	52
Teacher/lecturer prepares notes	30	34	18	82	41
Computer/laptop	30	15	5	50	25
Tape recorder/dictaphone	25	13	3	41	21
Friends take notes/ type up or borrow notes from friends	5	12	4	21	11
Use braille machine	16	2	-	18	9
Reader takes notes, prints or puts them on computer	8	5	2	15	8
Supply teacher/classroom assistant	6	6	-	12	6
Memory	3	5	2	10	5
Someone else takes them/ they get typed up/put onto computer	3	1	-	4	2
Someone else takes them while I dictate	2	-	-	2	1
Other methods	2	3	2	7	4
Total responses	**153**	**148**	**65**	**366**	**100**

n=199

Although most students used more than one method of taking notes, it can be seen that levels of vision had an effect on note-taking by looking at the three most frequently mentioned methods for each student group.

Students with very low vision (n=84):

- teacher or lecturer prepares notes: 36 per cent (over three in ten)
- use computer or laptop: 36 per cent (over three in ten)
- use tape-recorder or dictaphone: 30 per cent (three in ten).

Students with low vision (n=78):

- take them myself: 67 per cent (over six in ten)
- teacher or lecturer prepares notes: 44 per cent (over four in ten)
- use computer or laptop: 19 per cent (almost two in ten).

Students with high vision (n=37):

- take them myself: almost eight in ten
- teacher or lecturer prepares notes: almost five in ten
- use computer or laptop: more than one in ten.

This information from students indicates that the very low vision group were more dependent on technology or other people for their notes. The largest proportions of the other two groups took their own notes – over seven in ten of the low vision students and eight in ten of the high vision group. Over three in ten of the very low vision group made use of computers or laptops compared with around two in ten low vision students and over one in ten of the high vision students.

We were somewhat surprised by the extent to which some 27 per cent of students also relied on others' notes. In many cases, this may represent a short-term set of note-taking strategies, fixed on by students in the absence of adequate technological support or their own lack of note-taking skills. We wonder about the extent to which lectures are filtered through others' approaches to their content. Others will often not adhere to the same priorities and structuring of content which the blind and partially sighted students would if they had autonomy in the situation.

6.3 Examinations

6.3.1 Appropriate format examination papers

- One in ten students said they did not always get examination papers in their preferred format.

Students were asked whether they always received their examination papers in the format they wanted. In this question, students did not distinguish between public examinations, school or college set tests, 'mocks', or end of module tests, neither did they distinguish between examinations taken recently or those taken some time ago. Responses indicated that generally, students were examined via papers provided in their preferred format – nine out of ten FE students and eight out of ten sixth form and higher education students. Relatively few students – one in ten, in both mainstream and specialist education for blind and partially sighted students – said they did not always get examination papers in their preferred format. Though these proportions are low, this is a situation that should be addressed as a matter of urgency.

Results were very similar when looked at by visual level, as approximately eight in ten students in each of the three visual levels said they got their examination papers in their preferred formats. Thus we can conclude that the medium did not unduly affect these outcomes.

6.3.2 Late examination papers

- Four in ten sixth form and fewer than three in ten higher education students said they had received late examination papers on at least one occasion.
- Approximately one in ten of the FE college students had received late examination papers.

Students were asked whether their examination papers had arrived late on at least one occasion. Higher education students and sixth form students were more likely than FE college students to have received late exam papers. Four in ten sixth form and just under three in ten higher education students had received late exam papers, compared with just over one in ten of the FE college students. Those whose papers were late used a range of formats, including large print, braille, tape, disk and standard print.

When we analysed these data by level of vision, we noted that fewer of the very low vision students received late exam papers when compared with the other vision groups. Approximately one in five of the students with very low vision had received a late exam paper, compared with one in three of the students with low and high vision.

Of the 19 sixth form and FE students who had experience of late examination papers, 14 were in mainstream and five in specialist education. It therefore appears that, within this small sample, students in mainstream establishments were more likely than those in specialist placements to receive late exam papers.

6.3.3 Extra time for examinations

Because it takes longer to read and write braille and large print, blind and partially sighted students are usually granted additional time when taking examinations. The amount of additional time given varies from half the amount again, to double, or occasionally three times the amount for braillists. A factor to take into account is the length of the examination, as double time or more for long papers can be impractical and fatiguing. In reality, the additional time students need is a function of the medium they use and severity of their visual impairment, and is likely to vary from individual to individual.

Nine in ten sixth form and higher education students received extra time for their examinations, as did eight in ten FE college students.

6.3.4 Extra desk space for examinations

Large print and braille materials are bulkier than standard print materials. In an examination or test situation where students may have question papers, reference documents and answer sheets, as well as possibly a computer, brailler or other piece of access technology, some blind and partially sighted students will need more desk space than others. Most students in this research felt that they had the amount of desk space that they needed, although the large print users would all have liked more space.

Only eight of the 98 sixth form and FE students said they did not have enough desk space. Six of these were in mainstream education and two described their placement as "general specialist". In other words, all in specialist provision for blind and partially sighted students had enough desk space for examinations.

6.3.5 Lighting in examination rooms

Students were asked about the lighting in the examination room and how suitable it was for them. Similar proportions of students reported finding difficulties with lighting levels in exam rooms – one in ten sixth form and higher education students, and one in seven FE college students. While no differences were noted between specialist or mainstream provision, it was apparent that students with severe visual impairments were more likely than others to feel that the lighting level in their exam room was not suitable. For example, sixteen per cent of very low vision students were not happy with lighting levels, compared with eight per cent of those with low vision. All students with high vision said that the exam lighting suited them.

References

Richardson, J T E and Roy, A W N (2001). **The representation and attainment of students with a visual impairment in the United Kingdom.** Unpublished RNIB paper.

Roy, A W N (2001). **Student perspectives: discussions with visually impaired students on the effect of serious sight loss on themselves, their families, and friends.** RNIB: London.

CHAPTER SEVEN Equipment

Students were asked what equipment they used at home and at school or college. We also enquired about any additional equipment students felt they needed.

7.1 Computer use

- All but five students used computers.
- Six in ten used computers with magnification and more than four in ten used computers with speech output.

All but five students in this sample said that they used computers. Table 7.1 details the computers and specialist adaptations students used once a week or more, so some students have listed more than one type or adaptation. The percentages in the table are percentages of the whole sample who used a particular type of computer or adaptation, either at home, at their educational establishment or both.

Table 7.1 **Type of computer and adaptations used by students**

Type of computer used	At school, college or university		At home		Both home and educational establishment		Total	
	n	%	n	%	n	%	n	%
Normal screen	50	25	8	4	87	43	145	71
Magnification	33	16	22	11	35	17	123	61
Speech	23	11	14	7	34	17	94	46
Laptop	24	12	20	10	41	20	85	42
Large screen	32	16	25	12	26	12	83	41
Other	8	4	3	2	6	3	17	8

n=199

Table 7.1 shows that 71 per cent of students used a computer with a normal screen. Twenty five per cent of students used this only at school or college, four per cent used this only at home, while 43 per cent used it in both locations.

In addition, many students also used other adaptations. For example, 41 per cent used computers with a large screen and 61 per cent used computers with magnification. Forty six per cent of students used computers with speech output and 42 per cent of students used a laptop computer. Many of these students also had access to this equipment at home.

7.2 Equipment students needed but did not have

- Almost one student in five said they did not have access to some equipment they needed.

Students were asked whether there was any equipment they lacked and 19 per cent identified items they felt they needed.

Table 7.2 **Equipment students said they needed**

Equipment needed	Frequency
High tech equipment	
Computers	
Laptop computer	7
Computer for word processing	6
Computer with speech	4
Scanner (with computer)	4
Computer with magnification	1
Other high tech equipment	
CCTV	8
Optical character recognition (OCR) machine	3
Electronic brailler eg braille' n speak	2
Internet including modem	1
Braille embosser	1
Other specialist software, unspecified	1
CD-ROM (for reference purposes)	1
Low tech equipment	
Low vision aids or specialist low tech	
Perkins brailler	2
Magnifier	2
Monocular telescope	1
Laboratory equipment (specialist)	1
Kitchen utensils (specialist)	1
Everyday items or support	
Lamp	2
Tape recorder or dictaphone	1
Book stand	1
Plastic cover to remove paper glare	1

n=39 students

Table 7.2 shows that 22 of the 39 students said they needed computers with various specialist capabilities, such as scanners, magnification, or speech. Computers help blind and partially sighted people to access and participate in their education, often through adaptive technology, and we are concerned that so many of the students, 11 per cent of this sample, felt they still needed specific items. Seventeen students mentioned other high tech equipment that they needed, eight naming CCTVs. In the low technology and low vision aids section, a range of materials were identified, including magnifiers and specialist equipment to help with laboratory work on science courses and kitchen use on catering courses. These should all be relatively easy to provide. Six students mentioned everyday items that could very easily be obtained, such as a plastic cover to reduce glare and a lamp for task lighting.

The effect upon students of not having appropriate equipment is illustrated by the following comments from a student at FE college:

"I'd like to complete some work at home but it's so difficult to get equipment ie a laptop. I have got a computer but it is only small print. It would be helpful if they could help by giving a speech package. Large print package – it's so expensive."

Another student at sixth form college, speaking retrospectively about school, observed:

"…handouts were always late. I didn't have access to CCTVs so I couldn't research my school projects properly."

Of those students who needed equipment, approximately one in seven was at sixth form or FE college, and one in four at university. A mixture of high tech and low tech equipment was required by students in each group.

These 39 students explained why they did not have the equipment they felt they needed, some giving more than one reason.

Table 7.3 **Reasons for not having equipment needed**

Reasons for not having equipment needed	n
Cannot afford it	16
Did not know where to buy it	5
Waiting for it to arrive	5
Lack of advice about entitlement or waiting for assessment	5
Have not got round to buying it	4
Not provided	2
Did not know it was available	1
Immovable objects	1
Not essential enough to purchase	1
Would need training which is not available	1
Not compatible with current equipment	1
Do not want to become reliant on it	1

n=39

The commonest reason for not having equipment was the cost – over four in ten students mentioned this factor. Of the 16 students who said they did not have necessary equipment because of the cost, eight were at university or college of higher education, six were in sixth form or FE colleges and the remaining two students were at school. Table 7.4 gives a breakdown of the types of equipment these students felt was needed. School students expressed least need for additional items of equipment while students in higher education indicated the greatest need for additional items.

Table 7.4 **Equipment that students could not afford to buy**

Type of equipment needed	Current educational placement		
	University/ higher education	Sixth form/ FE college	School
	n	n	n
Modem	1	–	–
CD-ROM for reference	1	–	–
Computer for word processing	3	–	–
Monocular/telescope/ microscope	1	–	–
Electronic brailler (eg braille'n speak)	1	–	–
CCTV	1	–	–
Scanner (with computer)	–	1	–
Laptop computer	–	3	1
Computer with speech	–	2	–
Embosser	–	–	1
Total	**8**	**6**	**2**

n=39

The fact that a greater proportion of students in higher education indicated that they had not had an assessment of their special needs (see section 8.1) may also have a bearing on the numbers indicating that they did not have all the equipment they needed. Sixteen students who said they did not have all the equipment they needed had not had an assessment of their special needs before starting their course. Ten of these were in higher education, three were in FE and three were at sixth form college.

Five responses indicated that students were waiting for an assessment and five were simply waiting for new equipment to be delivered.

However ten students said they did not know where to buy the item, did not realise it was available, or had simply 'Not got round to buying it.'

One student said the item required was not compatible with their existing computer equipment, another indicated that training would be necessary (currently unavailable), while another said they did not want to become reliant on equipment. One student said that the extra item was desirable but not essential.

CHAPTER EIGHT Assessment and support

8.1 Assessment of students' special needs

- Seven in ten of the sixth form students and eight in ten FE college students had their learning needs assessed at the start of their course.
- Only six in ten of the higher education students had been assessed.
- Three in four of the mainstream students had their needs assessed at the start of their courses.
- The majority of students who had been assessed were satisfied with the assessment.

We asked whether students had received an assessment of their special needs at the start of their course, who had carried out the assessment, and whether they were satisfied with it. These questions were asked of all students apart from school sixth form students, as they would have received an assessment lower down the school. Table 8.1 presents this information.

Table 8.1 **Assessment of special needs**

Placement	Aware of their support needs	Assessed at start of course			Satisfied with assessment
		Yes	No	Unsure	
Sixth form college n=37	37	26	9	2	26 of 26
FE college n=69	61	55	12	2	54 of 55
Higher education n=76	70	48	28	-	42 of 48

n=182

All 37 sixth form college students who answered this question said they were aware of their learning needs at the start of their course, and so did the majority of FE and higher education students – approximately nine in ten. Seven in ten of the sixth form students and eight in ten FE college students had their learning needs assessed at the start of their course, but only six in ten of the higher education students had been assessed.

When we analysed the findings by mainstream and specialist placement, it appeared that nearly one in four of the 42 mainstream students and almost one in 10 of the 25 students at specialist establishments for blind and partially sighted students did not have their needs assessed at the start of their present courses.

All the sixth form students who had had an assessment said they were happy with it. Nine in ten FE and higher education students indicated that they were happy with their assessments. The few students who were not happy with their assessments gave the following reasons for this.

Table 8.2 **Reason for dissatisfaction with assessment**

Reason for dissatisfaction with assessment	Frequency
Inadequate or did not cover needs	4
Without equipment for a period or needed computer to take notes	2
Did not believe student had a problem	1
Student given notes of the assessment in an inaccessible format	1
Did not increase knowledge about needs.	1

n=7

8.1.1 Who carried out the assessment?

Students were asked who had carried out their assessment. Some students named more than one individual.

Table 8.3 **Staff involved in assessing students**

Who carried out assessment of learning needs?	Sixth form college n=35	FE college n=55	Higher education n=48	Total n=140	
	n	n	n	n	%
Member of staff at college eg tutor/other	8	37	13	58	41
Disability coordinator at college	11	16	17	44	31
Someone from RNIB	-	1	12	13	9
Member of staff from previous school or college	3	3	4	10	7
Other specialist VI workers from outside college	6	1	5	12	9
Social worker	1	2	2	5	4
Welfare adviser at college	1	-	2	3	2
Principal or vice principal at college	2	1	-	3	2
Other or not sure	3	2	5	7	5

Table 8.3 shows that students were assessed by a number of different people. The largest proportion of students were assessed by staff from within their college, either the disability coordinator or another member of staff. Those on higher education courses were more likely to use the services of RNIB for assessment – one in four had RNIB assessors, compared with only one student out of 55 in further education.

We are aware that recent advice and guidance for the post-16 education sector has been made available for staff who wish to improve the situation. Green and Bartram (1988), HEFCE (1999) and the Quality Assurance Agency for Higher Education (1999) all provide useful guidelines to staff which include drawing on other specialist assessment services as appropriate. Nevertheless, students, and especially those in transition, need to be made much more aware of their rights in this area, particularly in the context of new legislation (see Corlett, 2001).

8.2 Educational and social support

8.2.1 Support for students – whole group

- The majority of students felt they usually received the help they needed.
- Almost two in ten higher education students felt they did not have someone to talk to if they had a problem.

We were interested to find out whether our sample felt they had the support they needed to make the most of their time as students. There is more to this than educational support, as our questions reflected.

Table 8.4 **Did students feel they received the help and support they needed?**

Students who agreed with the following statements in the questionnaire	Sixth form school or college n=57 %	Further education college n=70 %	Higher education n=75 %
You usually get the help you need	84	77	78
If you have a problem, there is usually someone you can talk to	96	90	81
You sometimes get left out of social activities because of your sight difficulties	18	19	27
You sometimes avoid doing things that draw attention to your sight difficulties	40	32	49

n=202

Table 8.4 shows that more of the students in sixth forms agreed that they usually got the help they needed than students in further or higher education. More students in higher education agreed that they sometimes got left out of social activities and sometimes avoided doing things to draw attention to their sight difficulties, compared with those in sixth form and at further education colleges. However there are many factors affecting these data. For example, personality will have an effect on social aspects of education, as will students' living circumstances. Additionally, school and higher education are very different socially. Overall it was found that:

- just over eight out of ten sixth form students and just under eight out of ten of those in further and higher education college felt that they usually received the help they needed
- almost five out of ten of the higher education students agreed that they sometimes avoided doing things that drew attention to their sight difficulties, compared with four in ten of sixth form students and just over three in ten of the FE students
- almost three in ten students in higher education said they sometimes felt left out of social activities. However, personality variables may have had an impact here, as may the size of university or college campus, so it is not possible to draw firm conclusions from these data
- in comparison, fewer than two in ten of those at FE college and sixth form college sometimes felt left out of social activities
- almost two in ten higher education students felt they did not have someone to talk to if they had a problem, compared with fewer than one in ten FE college students, and only one in 20 sixth form students.

Feelings of social isolation may be more common among blind and partially sighted students in higher education. These findings lend some weight to the American research by Hodges and Keller (1999). This study and Appelhans' (1993) findings emphasised the need to develop social skills in blind and partially sighted pupils to assist their future inclusion in campus life. Further, McBroom (1997) reported that one third of 102 blind and partially sighted higher education students took no part in extra-curricular social activities. To some extent, personality factors may be coming into play in our findings but so too will issues such as social skills and the additional time taken simply to do coursework, which reduces the time available for socialising.

8.2.2 Support in mainstream and specialist education

- More students in specialist placements felt supported than did mainstream students.

Responses from sixth form and FE college students were examined together to see if there were differences depending on whether students attended mainstream or specialist education. The data below show that while differences were smaller, more students in specialist placements felt supported than did mainstream students:

- over nine in ten of those students in specialist placements for blind and partially sighted students felt that they usually received the help they needed
- over eight in ten mainstream students said they usually received the help they needed.

There was little difference between mainstream and specialist students in terms of having someone to talk to if they had a problem. For both groups, approximately nine in ten students said they had someone to talk to.

Slightly higher proportions of mainstream students in our sample said they sometimes felt left out of social activities:

- three in ten mainstream students said they sometimes felt left out of social activities
- only one in ten of the students in specialist provision said that they sometimes felt left out.

Unsurprisingly, students who had a big group of friends were less likely to say that they did not have someone to talk to about their problems than students who said they did not have many friends. Of the 60 students who did not have a big group of friends, one in five said that they did not usually have someone to talk to about their problems, compared with fewer than one in ten of the 144 who had a big group of friends. Similarly, 16 per cent of the 74 who wished that they had more friends did not usually have someone to talk to about their problems, compared with eight per cent of the 127 who did not wish they had more friends.

8.2.3 Avoiding drawing attention to sight difficulties

There was little difference between mainstream and specialist students in terms of avoiding drawing attention to their sight difficulties. Approximately half the students in both groups said that they sometimes avoided drawing attention to their sight difficulties.

8.2.4 Support and levels of vision

The same questions were explored in relation to participants' levels of vision. When compared with the students who had high vision, slightly more of those with low or very low vision said they did not get all the help they needed, or always had someone to talk to if they had a problem. These differences, however, were relatively minor. There was a more pronounced difference in social activities – one in three of the students with very low vision said they sometimes felt left out, compared with one in five of the students with low vision and only one out of the 37 students with high vision. Almost half of the students said they sometimes avoided drawing attention to their sight difficulties, with no difference associated with level of vision.

8.3 Overall support

- Almost eight in ten students felt that they received the support they needed overall.
- Students with either very low or low vision were least likely to feel that they had all the support that they needed – only six in ten compared with nine in ten of those with high vision.

Students were asked whether, overall, they felt they received the support they needed at their place of learning to be able to undertake their studies to the best of their ability.

Table 8.5 **Support students received**

Support students received	Sixth form		Further education		Higher education	
	n	%	n	%	n	%
Received support overall	48	84	56	80	55	73
Did not receive support overall	9	16	13	19	20	26
Unsure	-	-	1	1	1	1
Total	**57**	**100**	**70**	**100**	**76**	**100**

n=203

Table 8.5 shows that, among all these students, over eight in ten felt that they received the support they needed overall. Eight in ten of the FE college students and just under seven in ten of the students in higher education felt well supported. Just over one in four of those at university or higher education college felt that they did not get all the support they needed.

We analysed the sixth form and FE college students' responses to find out whether attending mainstream or specialist provision made any difference. Although the majority of students felt supported overall, the proportion was slightly higher in specialist establishments. While eight in ten mainstream students felt that they got the support they needed, nearly nine in ten specialist students felt this way.

We found a larger difference in responses when we analysed students' answers by their visual level. While nine in ten of the students whose vision was categorised as high felt supported, only six in ten for those with either very low or low vision felt that they had all the support that they needed.

Students who felt they had not received the support they needed were asked the reasons for this. Reasons given were similar across the three student groups, and so are presented together. The 42 students who responded represent 21 per cent of all of those sampled.

Table 8.6 **Reasons students gave for not feeling supported**

Reasons students gave for feeling they did not get the support needed	n
Not enough help or individual attention	21
Lack of awareness by department or institution	13
Lack of specialist staff	9
Problems with equipment	8
Refusal by staff to recognise disability or ways around it	7
Lack of recognition of extra time required for studies	6
Time taken to get notes into appropriate format	6
More materials in right format	3
Chose not to receive support	1

n=42

The table shows that about half of the students who did not feel supported believed they did not receive enough individual attention, as illustrated by the following quotes:

"Teachers do not go out of their way to assist me. [Need] more one to one teaching. Better understanding of the work I'm given. Assistance from special needs teacher."

Student, aged 25, talking about HE college

"...I had to fight. I did not get extra time. I had a lot of problems with lecturers. When I said that I couldn't see the blackboard, they would write things bigger which didn't help. Course notes where in too small print. This was constant."

23 year-old student talking about university

"They only help if they have time. You have to do most things for yourself. They don't give me extensions for coursework."

20 year-old student talking about university

Almost one in three believed that there was a lack of awareness of their needs on the part of the department or establishment:

"University is not aware of the level of support I need. I wasn't totally ready for it either. It was my first encounter with mainstream. People's fear of disability...either prioritise or avoid."

21 year-old student talking about university

".... so many students at university and you have so many different lecturers. Then they change and cannot remember individual needs. No departmental awareness."

20 year-old student talking about university

"Teachers are not qualified to deal with pupils with sight difficulties. They have never had the experience of teaching those pupils before – don't understand my needs, eg I have to wait for handouts when I need them for a specific class."

18 year-old student, talking about FE college

Approximately one in five students said that there was a lack of specialist staff as well as problems with equipment:

"No braille service. Handouts not in appropriate format. No central coordinating policy for visually impaired students – experience can vary from one academic department to another."

23 year-old student talking about university

References

Appelhans, P (1993). **Integration of visually impaired students.** European Journal of Special Needs Education, 8.

Corlett, S (2001). **SEN and Disability Bill.** The Skill Journal, 69.

Green, M and Bartram, D (1998). **Initial assessment to identify learning needs.** Further Education Development Agency.

Higher Education Funding Councils for England and Wales (1999). **Guidance on base-level provision for disabled students in higher education institutions.** HEFCE and HEFCW: Cambridge.

Hodges, J S and Keller, M J (1999). **Visually impaired students' perception of their social integration in college.** Journal of Visual Impairment and Blindness 93 AFB, New York.

McBroom, L W (1997). **Making the grade: college students with visual impairments.** Journal of Visual Impairment and Blindness, 91 AFB, New York.

Quality Assurance Agency for Higher Education (1999). **Code of practice for the assurance of academic quality and standards in higher education: section 3 students with disabilities.** QAA: Gloucester.

CHAPTER NINE Careers advice and work experience

Most young people who go into further or higher education do so because they wish either to pursue a chosen career path or to maximise their career options. This chapter explores their preparation for work and their career aspirations.

9.1 Careers advice

- Over nine in ten students had received careers advice.

Ninety six per cent of students participating in the survey had received careers advice at some point. Of the eight students who had received none, six were in higher education and two were in further education – one in mainstream and one at a specialist college for blind and partially sighted students. We were concerned that students had reached this stage without apparently having received any careers advice. When these students were asked if they would have liked careers advice, four would have welcomed it, three would not, and one did not know.

9.1.1 Source of careers advice

Of the 196 students who had received careers advice, the majority (88 per cent) had received this from a careers adviser at school. Ten per cent of students had not received careers advice at school, and three students (two per cent) were unsure whether they had or not.

Of the 10 per cent (n=21) of students who had not received careers advice when at school, 15 had gone to mainstream schools, three of which had a specialist resource base for blind and partially sighted pupils; three had been at special school for blind and partially sighted students and three had attended both mainstream and special schools.

Students were also asked whether they had received careers advice from a source other than the school careers officer. Sixty-five per cent had, 32 per cent had not, and one student was unsure.

Table 9.1 **Source of careers advice**

Source of careers advice	n	%
At school and from another source	112	59
At school only	59	31
From another source and not at school	18	9
From another source and unsure about whether advised at school	2	1
Total who received advice	**191**	**100**

Table 9.1 shows that the largest proportion of students (59 per cent) had received careers advice both at school and from another source, while 31 per cent had received advice at school only. Nine per cent had received advice from another source and not at school. Two students (one per cent) had received other advice and were unsure whether they had received advice at school or not. Those students who had said that they had received careers advice from another source were asked who had given them advice. The details of these different sources are given in table 9.2.

Table 9.2 **Other sources of careers advice**

Source of advice	n	%
General careers adviser	64	48
Teacher or lecturer	43	33
Member of family	39	30
Special needs careers adviser	32	24
Friend(s)	23	17
RNIB student adviser	10	8
Staff at job centre or job club	9	7
Social worker	1	<1
Other	12	9

n=132

Several sources of careers advice were mentioned. Forty eight per cent had had advice from a general careers adviser and 24 per cent from a "special needs" careers adviser. Teachers and lecturers played an important role in advising students, with 33 per cent receiving advice from this source. Family members advised 30 per cent of the students. This is considerably lower than Keys et al (1998) found in their sample of non-disabled students, where the largest proportion said they had received careers advice from parents or guardians – 56 per cent of FE college students and 69 per cent of sixth form students. Friends were a source of advice for 17 per cent of students in our research. Only eight per cent (n=10) of the 132 students who said they had received advice from another source named an RNIB student adviser.

9.1.2 Satisfaction with advice received

- More than eight in ten students were generally satisfied with the careers advice received.

Students were asked how satisfied they were with the careers advice they had received. Of the 191 students who answered this question, 84 per cent (n=160) were generally satisfied. Students who had said they were not satisfied were asked for the reasons. Several students gave more than one reason.

Table 9.3 **Dissatisfaction with careers advice**

Reasons for dissatisfaction with careers advice	n
Not helpful	15
Lack of understanding on part of the adviser	8
Told to do or pushed into something they were not interested in	8
Range of careers not explored	6
Told they could not do jobs they knew they could	5
Used a computer assisted program	3
Changed career plans since given the advice	3
Extra courses or training felt to be unnecessary	3
Lack of information on handout, small print	3
Other	6

n=29

As table 9.3 shows, 15 of the 29 students who were dissatisfied had simply found the advice unhelpful:

"I found it far too vague - no direction offered."

FE student aged 17

"I wasn't really sure what I wanted to do. They did not give me a plan of action of what I should do next. No handouts or leaflets."

Sixth form student aged 16

Generally regarded as unhelpful was the adviser's use of a computer-assisted program. This was specifically mentioned by three students.

"Not helpful in any way. You tick boxes and send it away. All information was put into a computer and what you are most compatible with, ie your most suited career, is suggested. It was suggested I work in a laboratory or as a teacher. This was not suitable."

University student aged 18

"They just give you a computer print out and don't really help you at all."

Sixth form college student aged 17

Eight students felt that they were pushed towards jobs or training they considered unsuitable or unnecessary, as illustrated by the following comment:

"I felt that for going to the places I wanted to pursue, I was discouraged. Types of training places, courses suggested were not suitable to my needs but when I said this to the careers adviser, he didn't like this."

FE student aged 23

"Range of careers wasn't explored. I was geared towards secretarial work which is what I ended up doing...."

University student, age not given

" I was told that I could not do certain jobs when I could do them – management, things like that. Generally I was told I could be a secretary."

University student aged 18

9.1.3 Expectations of others

- A third of students had been told they could not do a job they were interested in because of their sight difficulties.

Students were asked if they had ever been told they could not do a job they wanted to do in the future because of their sight difficulties and 34 per cent of students (n=69) said they had been discouraged for that reason. It is important to remember here that these sections are reporting the student's perception of the outcome of the careers interview and there may have been occasions when a student was advised against a particular career choice for many different reasons, but the student inferred that their visual impairment was a factor.

Among the careers students said they had been advised against were occupations with a substantial practical element, such as carpentry, catering, horticulture, acting and teaching, as well as a variety of other jobs including police work, posts in ICT, medicine, accountancy, psychiatry and architecture.

While some students' career choices may well have been inappropriate, such as, for example, six who were interested in jobs as drivers and one who had wanted to be a footballer, most of the other occupations could well be pursued by a blind or partially sighted person, given the right training and support. It is difficult to understand fully why some students were discouraged from applying to take up office, clerical and administrative work, for example, given modern technology.

We asked students who had told them they could not do a job they had expressed an interest in. They gave the following responses which are detailed in table 9.4.

Table 9.4 **Who had discouraged students from certain jobs**

Person who had told student they could not do a job they were interested in	Frequency
Special needs adviser	17
Teacher/lecturer	13
General careers adviser	11
Family member	9
Health worker	7
Members of their chosen profession	4
Staff member on their work experience	4
Friends	4
Other response	14
Total	**83**

n=69

These findings suggest that much needs to be done by way of informing careers and specialist careers advisers about the opportunities that exist in so many areas of employment today for blind and partially sighted people.

9.1.4 **Best source of careers advice**

Students were asked who they believed had given them the best careers advice. Although 112 students had received advice from more than one source, 103 named their best source of advice and nine students did not consider one source better than another.

Table 9.5 **Source of students' best careers advice**

Source of students' best advice	n	%
General careers adviser, including college adviser	27	26
Special needs careers adviser	14	14
Careers adviser at school	14	14
Teacher/lecturer	13	13
All helped equally	13	13
Family member	9	9
RNIB student adviser	4	4
Found out myself	3	3
Friend	2	2
Staff at job club/job centre	1	1
Not sure	3	3

n=103

One student in four who expressed a preference named the general careers adviser (including the careers adviser at college) as their best source of advice, while one in seven named the special needs careers adviser, and the same number cited the careers adviser at school and their teacher/lecturer. Family members played an important role, with almost one in ten of the students identifying a member of their family as their best source of careers advice. Only four students selected the RNIB student adviser out of the ten who had had this support.

9.1.5 The best time to receive careers advice

Students were asked when they felt was the best time to receive careers advice. They suggested the key times for intervention (indicated by the greatest number of responses) were just before leaving secondary school (n=34), during the final year at school (n=33), and before choosing options for GCSEs. There were numerous other replies detailing every possible stage of the education process. Forty five students gave the responses "anytime", "ongoing" or "when needed by the individual", suggesting that while there may be key stages for intervention, an individualistic approach was best.

Some comparisons can be made to other recent research by RNIB. Simkiss, Garner and Dryden (1988) report other weaknesses in the careers guidance process. Their study revealed that blind and partially sighted students on particular courses (access courses, clerical skills, computing) were very unlikely to receive any careers guidance at all. The likelihood of guidance rose to 50 per cent for students studying business and finance, leisure, and teacher training. Their study applied a more stringent criterion than the present research. They asked whether students had actually received careers guidance when they badly needed it, regardless of whether they had received any guidance previously. In many cases, the answer was negative.

9.2 Job search skills

- Over seven in ten students had been trained to write CVs.
- Only one in five had been trained to find out about job vacancies.

Students were asked about the training they had received in finding out about job vacancies, filling in job application forms, preparing curriculum vitae (CVs) and in interview skills.

The following percentages of the whole student group indicated that they had had such training.

Table 9.6 **Job search skills**

Job finding skills	Training received %	Have experience of %	Feel confident doing %
Finding out about job vacancies	20	44	51
Filling in job application forms	36	52	50
Writing CVs	74	73	60
Interview skills	45	47	52

n=204

Seventy four per cent of students had received training in writing CVs and 60 per cent felt confident in writing them. However, only 20 per cent of students received training in finding out about job vacancies, although 44 per cent of students had experience of doing this and 51 per cent of the students felt confident about searching out vacancies. Fewer than half of the students had received training in interview skills, which is an area where initial impressions are crucial; however, 52 per cent of students felt confident in their interview skills.

A relatively high proportion of students had had experience of all of the above, bearing in mind that these students were still in full-time education. While just over half of the students felt confident in all four areas, that still leaves a considerable number of students who did not. Blind and partially sighted job seekers are already at a disadvantage in a competitive labour market, so it is vital for them to be equipped with the skills needed to succeed.

9.3 Experience of work

Table 9.7 shows the proportions of students who had held or applied for a job, either part-time, full-time or unpaid voluntary work.

Table 9.7 **Experience of paid or voluntary employment**

Employment experience	Full-time paid job n=198 %	Part-time paid job n=201 %	Unpaid voluntary work n=194 %
Yes	15	43	58
No, but have applied	15	6	3
No, and have not applied	70	51	39

The numbers with experience of full-time employment were relatively low at 15 per cent, which is the same for those who had applied for full-time employment. This is to be expected, as these students were either in or had just left full time education. Some will have undertaken full-time paid work during vacations. Forty three per cent of the sample had experience of part-time paid work, and 58 per cent of the sample had done unpaid voluntary work. Six per cent of students said they had applied for part-time employment, and three per cent had applied without success for unpaid voluntary work.

Twenty four per cent (n=48) of the students in the sample had a paid job of some sort at the time of the survey. No gender differences were found, but when explored by age, it was found that a larger proportion of those under the age of 19 had some paid work compared with those over 19. Thirty two per cent of those under 19 had paid work, compared with 16 per cent of these over the age of 19 (n=101 in each group).

In total, 68 per cent of students in our sample had experienced some form of work on either a paid or voluntary basis, including those who were in paid employment at the time of the survey.

9.3.1 Experience of paid employment and level of vision

- Students with the lowest levels of vision were least likely to have had paid work.

When we analysed paid employment by level of vision, we found that fewer students in the lower vision level categories reported having had a job. Of those students with very low vision (n=84), one in ten reported that they had had a job, compared with two in ten of the 78 students with very low vision and five in ten of the 37 students with the highest vision.

These results strike us as quite depressing. Why is it that students with more severe sight loss are so unlikely to be benefiting from any paid employment? It could be that time taken to process coursework, including preparatory work for the next year of a course, eats into possible employment time to the point where it becomes untenable. Despite this, however, we suspect that all too often blind and partially sighted students are simply denied equal access to employment opportunities. For instance, how often do college and university careers services make a genuine effort to ensure equal access to casual vacancy information? Many blind and partially sighted students cannot access job advertisements pinned on notice boards or information located in files within careers libraries. Careers guidance in its widest sense is a college and university service already covered by the Disability Discrimination Act (1995) and staff are required to make reasonable adjustments to ensure an equal opportunity for all students with disabilities.

9.3.2 Work experience

Students were asked how they obtained their work experience at school, college or university, and who had arranged it.

Table 9.8 **Who had arranged work experience**

Work experience	n	%
At school arranged by self	102	50
At school arranged by someone else	131	65
At college or higher education arranged by self	47	23
At college or higher education arranged by someone else	56	28

n=203

Note: several students had had more than one kind of work experience.

Clearly a greater proportion of students had work experience at school (whether arranged by themselves or by someone else) than they did subsequently at college when around half as many had employment experience.

9.3.3 Views on work experience

- Students had favourable views of work experience: more than eight in ten thought it had taught them new skills.

Those who had some work experience were asked whether they felt they had learned new skills from it and whether they felt more confident as a result. Generally, students had a favourable impression of their work experience. Table 9.9 shows the percentage of students who agreed with various statements about their work experience.

Table 9.9 **Students' views of work experience**

Statements about work experience	Agree %
Learned new skills	86
It is likely to be good preparation for when you get a job	77
Boosted self-confidence	78
Was generally well treated by work colleagues	98
Was generally well treated by boss	96

n=194

Nearly all the students who had had work experience felt that they had been well treated by their colleagues and by their boss. Eighty six per cent said that they had learned new skills on their work experience. A lesser proportion (77 per cent) felt that their work experience was likely to be good preparation for when they got a job. This is probably due to the fact that the type of job done as work experience can be very different from what students ultimately want to do.

9.3.4 Jobs students were doing when surveyed

Those who had paid employment at the time of the survey were employed in a range of jobs, presented in table 9.10.

Table 9.10 **Students' employment at the time of the survey**

Job	n
Shop work/supermarket work	13
Bar/hotel work	7
Office/administration	3
Paper round/milk round	3
Receptionist	2
Working with children/babysitting	2
Gardening	2
Sales	2
More than one job/agency work	5
Other: Trainee actuary, working with animals, musician, apprentice, working from home	8

n=47

9.4 Career aspirations

- The majority of students of average learning ability in our survey were aiming for professional careers.
- Almost nine in ten who stated a preferred occupation thought they would achieve their career goals.

We also asked students about the job they would like to do when they had completed their education. Table 9.11 represents their career aspirations. Many students were aiming for professional careers; this is not surprising as all the students in the survey sample were in non-compulsory further or higher education.

Table 9.11 **Jobs students would like to do after leaving education**

Occupation	Frequency
Office/clerical	**13**
Admin/typist/office/clerical/PA	10
Working for government/council	3
Arts/crafts	**21**
Music/DJ/sound engineer	10
Acting/performing arts/entertainment	5
Writer/author	2
Design (unspecified)	2
Artist/photographer	2
Retail/catering/services to people	**22**
Leisure/travel industry	8
Working with people/young people/blind and partially sighted people	3
Hairdressing	2
Babysitting/childminding	2
Chef/catering	2
Publican	1
Classroom assistant	1
Work in shop	1
Professional	**93**
Computers/IT/web design/software engineer	30
Teacher	18
Caring profession eg social work, nurse, counselling	13

continued on next page

Lawyer/solicitor/barrister	6
Finance/actuary/accountant/insurance	5
Physiotherapist/occupational therapist	4
Manager/businessperson	4
Physiology/chemistry/laboratory worker	3
Doctor	2
Interpreter/languages	2
Speech therapist	2
Geologist/archaeologist	2
Scientist	1
Vet	1
Media	**13**
Media/journalism	9
Advertising/PR	2
Marketing/sales	2
Factory/manual/practical	**8**
Trade eg mechanic/machinist	6
Gardening/horticulture	2
Other responses	
Other occupations	5
Not sure/unspecified	27

n=204

Of the 174 students who had stated a preferred occupation, 89 per cent thought they would end up doing this job, showing high levels of determination and ambition. Four per cent thought they would not, and seven per cent were unsure.

All 19 students who had said they would not end up in their chosen job or were unsure gave a reason for saying so and four students gave two reasons. As can be seen from the list below, eight students gave reasons directly related to their sight (one gave two sight-related reasons), the rest were either not related or not directly related to their sight:

- six students said their sight problems would make it difficult, as would lack of suitable equipment
- five were not completely decided on their career
- four said it was hard to get into their chosen profession (one wanted to go into the performing arts, two into music/sound recording/disc-jockeying and one wanted to work for local government/council)
- three said they had no experience, and would need qualifications
- three expressed concern that they might experience prejudice from employers because of their sight
- one student (who wanted to get into computing/IT) said they would have to move to achieve their ambition
- one student said they could not get to job interviews.

References

Keys, W, Maychell, K with Evans, C, Brooks, R, Lee, B and Pathak, S (1998). **Staying on. A study of young people's decisions about school sixth forms, sixth form-colleges and colleges of further education.** National Foundation for Educational Research, Berkshire.

Simkiss, P, Garner, S and Dryden G (1998). **What next? The experience of transition: visually impaired students, their education and preparation for employment.** RNIB, London.

Disability Discrimination Act (1995). Stationery Office, London.

CHAPTER 10 **The future**

The final section in the questionnaire addressed students' hopes and ambitions for the future. In general, students had high ambitions for their careers and expressed similar desires for their future as would any group of disabled or non-disabled young people – that is, to do well, be happy and live independently. Students wanted to reduce discrimination and disadvantage for others in the future.

10.1 **Personal ambitions**

Of 204 students, 56 per cent (115) said they had personal ambitions, some of which are listed below; 42 of these students had two ambitions, 20 named three:

Table 10.1 **Ambitions for the future: blind and partially sighted young people aged 16 to 25**

Ambition	Number of males (n=67)	Number of females (n=48)	All (n=115) %*
Get a job (general or specific)/ do well in a job	28	11	34
Travel/experience different cultures	17	10	23
Enjoy/make the most of life/ be happy	5	9	12
Get married	6	7	11
Have children	3	9	10
Do well in examinations (academic or non-academic)	6	4	9
House of my own/better house	4	3	6
Go to college/university	1	5	5

To live somewhere else	3	3	5
Enough money to live well	4	2	5
Do voluntary work with clubs/ organisations	2	4	5
Sporting ambitions	5	1	5
Start own business	3	2	4
Improvement in vision	3	–	3
Do something adventurous	2	3	4
Have the same opportunities as others	1	2	3
To live independently	1	3	3
Not let others stop me	–	2	2
Other	5	1	5

*Note: the percentages are based on the number of people who answered this question rather than upon the number of responses. The percentage column therefore exceeds 100 per cent.

It is readily apparent that, between them, this sample of blind and partially sighted young people had a wide range of ambitions for the future. Like many of their generation, almost one in four (27 young people) wanted to travel and to experience other cultures. A further five young people simply expressed a wish to do "something adventurous".

One in three (39 respondents) said they would like to get a job or do well in a job; and some said there was a specific job they wanted to do. If we consider these 39 young people in addition to the 88 who said their only ambition was to get a certain type of job, out of the total sample (203 respondents), over three in five (63 per cent per cent) cited finding work as one of their future aims. A further five young people expressed an aim to start their own business.

One in ten respondents said they would like to get married and a further one in ten said it was their ambition to have children in the future; although fewer males (one in 25) than females (one in five) listed parenthood among their aims for the future.

One in ten young people simply stated a wish to enjoy or make the most of life, or to be happy. Gender differences were again found (approximately one in 14 males compared with one in five females), although the numbers are too small for this to be generalised to the population as a whole.

Other ambitions were, again, similar to those to be expected among any group of young people in this age range; these included a wish to do well in their examinations, to go to college or university, to have their own home, and to have enough money to live well.

A minority of young people, however, cited aims that were – or could be – directly linked to their sight:

- three young people wanted their eyesight to improve
- three asked for the same opportunities as other (sighted) young people
- two said their aim was to "not let others stop them"
- four wished to live independently (only one of these young people had other disabilities in addition to their sight difficulty).

10.2 What needs to change?

- More than one in three students wanted to see changes in attitudes towards blind and partially sighted people.
- Almost one in three students wanted better support in education.
- More than one student in five wanted more information in a format they could read.

Students were also asked to list three things that they would like to change in order to improve the lives of children and young people with sight difficulties. Not surprisingly, themes that emerged focused around attitudes of others, the available social and economic support, support within education, and access to materials in accessible formats. Two hundred and three students answered this question:

Table 10.2 **What blind and partially sighted young people aged 16 to 25 would like to change to make life better for children and young people with sight difficulties (multiple responses up to a maximum of three)**

Things that would make life better	All young people %
Better attitudes/understanding by other people of the needs of blind and partially sighted children and young people	35
Better support in school and college/better training for teachers in needs of blind and partially sighted students	31
Greater availability of material in accessible formats	22
Improved public transport/better facilities to aid pedestrians	18
More opportunities for blind and partially sighted people	13
More help or support for daily living	12
More awareness of/contact with outside world	12
More services/provision for blind and partially sighted people	9
More/better equipment for blind and partially sighted people	8
Leisure facilities/play areas/sports and social activities	8
Medical advances	7
More/better information generally for blind and partially sighted children and young people	6
Improved mobility and independence	6
Better job prospects for blind and partially sighted people	4
More financial support/benefits information	4
Better careers/job seeking/FE and higher education entry advice	4

Things that would make life better	All young people %
Better physical access to places	4
More useful computers/wider availability of technology	2
Better laws to protect rights of disabled children	2
More support/understanding for blind and partially sighted children and families	2
Support groups/other blind and partially sighted people to talk to	2
Other	3
Not sure	6

n=203

Note: the percentages are based on the number of respondents who answered this question rather than upon the total number of responses. The total in the percentage column therefore exceeds 100 per cent.

The item which ranked highest was an appeal for an improvement in attitudes of other people towards children and young people with sight difficulties, with just over one in three (35 per cent) choosing this.

The second highest-ranking item – mentioned by just under one in three respondents (31 per cent) – was a request for better support in schools and colleges for blind and partially sighted students, including improved training for mainstream teachers. Many older students had been very forthcoming in their comments on the lack of support received at school, college or university, as this example demonstrates:

"The general atmosphere at the college was unfriendly, a bit awkward and the teachers didn't communicate enough to me about my sight problems. I

had a person who would have a short chat to me every couple of weeks to see how things were going. I guess he could have reported back but I didn't find that helpful. I would have preferred the teachers to have spoken to me."
Sixth form college student aged 16

Perhaps as a reflection of their own needs for independence, and dissatisfaction with public transport and general access to public places, 18 per cent of students cited improved public transport, information about public transport, or facilities to aid pedestrians as features that would be helpful. A further 6 per cent said that improved mobility and independence education would help many young people with sight difficulties, and 4 per cent (eight respondents) asked specifically for better physical access to public places.

Interestingly, only 4 per cent of young people listed better job prospects for people with sight difficulties, although this ranked highest for the primary and secondary groups. A further 4 per cent of older students however, requested better advice about careers, job-seeking and entry to further and higher education, and 13 per cent (more than one in ten) asked for more opportunities generally for blind and partially sighted people.

One in ten (12 per cent) said that more contact with the outside world would make life better for blind and partially sighted children and young people, a reference, perhaps, to a feeling of being excluded from mainstream society. A higher proportion of students who were currently (or in the case of university students, had previously been) in specialist education cited this as an improvement – 16 per cent of those who were or had been in specialist education compared with 7 per cent in mainstream schools or colleges. Social exclusion can affect a blind or partially sighted young person's self-confidence and ability to acquire the social skills necessary to participate fully in wider society. In addition, as the following observations suggest, if visually impaired and sighted people lack opportunities to meet in an everyday context, negative and/or false stereotypes about blind and partially sighted people cannot be challenged. This is, of course, closely linked to the issue of other people's attitudes towards blind and partially sighted children and young people.

"Many people don't come into contact with blind people to break down barriers."

Female student aged 18

Other ways in which respondents felt that the lives of children and young people with sight difficulties could be improved may be broadly placed into two categories. These were:

- services, facilities, activities and equipment suitable for blind and partially sighted children and young people (27 per cent in total)
- better support and information for blind and partially sighted children, young people and their families (8 per cent overall).

Taken together, the young people's responses to this question indicate that the over-riding need is for a far greater awareness among ordinary people, as well as those employed in specific areas, such as education, leisure and transport, about the capabilities and needs of blind and partially sighted children and young people. Full social inclusion means that services and amenities are automatically made accessible for blind and partially sighted people as a right, and not as a concession. A greater public understanding of sight problems would, it is hoped, lead to an acceptance of blind and partially sighted people as ordinary members of society, whose particular needs are taken for granted as part of everyday life. Once this is achieved, blind and partially sighted young people would no longer feel that they were regarded as "some sort of alien", but would be accepted on their individual merits, as requested by this young man:

"People being more willing to accept me as I am and me not having to prove myself as a member of the group."

University student aged 21

PART THREE

Students with visual impairment and additional learning difficulties

CHAPTER ELEVEN Background

We used a variety of approaches to investigate the educational experiences of blind and partially sighted students with complex needs including learning difficulties aged between 16 to 25.

11.1 The young people involved in the survey

Although we were keen throughout the research to ask the young people themselves about their lives and experiences, this was not a realistic option for all of the students with more severe learning difficulties. While eight of the students with moderate learning difficulties completed written questionnaires themselves, nine others answered the same range of questions in telephone interviews, allowing the interviewer to explain or simplify the wording when necessary. (Eight of the parents of students with moderate learning difficulties completed complementary questionnaires.) Twenty six parents of young people with moderate or severe learning difficulties who were unable to answer the questions themselves completed questionnaires on behalf of their children.

The range of questions in the parent and young person's questionnaires differed significantly as each could comment on different aspects of the student's education. While a parent knew of the reasoning behind the choice of a student's school or college and the range of provision available, for example, the student knew more about using facilities at school or college. Thus some questions were part of a subset of studies: we only asked students with moderate learning difficulties about their experience of careers advice, for instance.

As a result of these sub-groups of parents and young people, we received a very small number of responses to many questions. While our sample contains 43 young people with visual impairment and learning difficulties, only the 17 students with moderate learning difficulties who completed their own questionnaires were asked about careers advice and only the 34 parents of the more disabled students were asked about the choice of schools and colleges. Clearly, we cannot generalise from these small samples but they reveal a range of issues concerning the education of young people over the age of 16 with visual impairment and learning difficulties and serve to highlight the diversity of the educational needs of this group.

All of these young people had impairments in addition to their sight. As individuals, they differed widely in their abilities, levels of vision and degrees of independence. The students' educational experiences were also varied, and from this small sample it is not possible to draw general conclusions. However, as observations on their educational experiences, these data provide valuable insight into the challenges faced by the students and by their parents.

11.2 Functional vision

We asked parents of students with severe and moderate learning difficulties if the young person could see where the window was located in a room and about their preferences for specific lighting conditions to determine whether they had "high" or "low" vision. It emerged that the majority of the students were able to identify where the window was located and more than two in five had a specific lighting condition which they preferred:

- 22 of the 33 students for whom information was available could see where the window was in a room
- of the 31 students for whom information was available, 12 preferred bright light, seven had no preference and eight preferred dim light. Three of the students did not have any light perception and the parent of one student was unsure.

Using this information, 22 of the students' visual levels were recorded as "high" while the remaining seven were identified as "low".

11.3 Parents' and students' descriptions of vision

From the 37 responses received, it emerged that the term "partially sighted" was the most widely used to describe the young people's vision:

- 14 young people described themselves or were described by their parents as "partially sighted"
- seven respondents indicated that the student was "visually impaired"
- six respondents described the student as "blind"
- four respondents indicated that the young person was "unable to see very well"

- four students were said to have a "sight difficulty"
- one student said that they used the term poor eyesight to describe their visual difficulties and one parent explained that their child required surgery to "correct their vision".

11.4 Additional disabilities

Between them, parents named 67 disabilities their children had in addition to a visual impairment. The most common conditions parents gave included epilepsy (7), cerebral palsy (5), Downs Syndrome (5), and an unspecified learning disability (5). These disabilities were similar to those most commonly found among the children with additional complex difficulties aged between 5 and 16 in our survey, reported in Crofts et al (2001), Report 5 of this series.

Reference

Crofts, K, Clery, L, Keil, S, Franklin, A and Cole-Hamilton, I (2001). **The health and well-being of blind and partially sighted children and young people aged 5 to 25.** RNIB, London.

CHAPTER TWELVE Type and choice of educational placements and courses

In this chapter, we analyse students' current educational placements and the reason for that choice. We also asked whether their placement was full or part time, day or residential, and the type and length of their course. The range of subjects they were studying and any qualifications they hoped to gain were also investigated.

12.1 Students' current educational placements

- Young people with the most severe disabilities were most likely to be in specialist education.

Similar numbers of the young people in our sample were studying at schools and at colleges; 21 were still at school and the remaining 16 were at college. Students were more likely to be in general special needs or specialist provision for blind and partially sighted students than in a mainstream setting:

- 14 of the school students were in general specialist provision.

One student was in a special school with an further education unit, four attended special schools for blind and partially sighted students and three were in mainstream schools, one of which was linked to a special school:

- of those college students whose type of provision was specified, seven were in specialist colleges for blind and partially sighted students, five were in general specialist provision and three were in mainstream colleges. One gave no details.

All of the students attending mainstream schools and colleges had moderate learning difficulties and this reflects our finding about the younger age group of children with additional complex needs (aged 5 to 16) that more of those with the least severe difficulties attended mainstream placements. This is reported fully in Report 2 of this series (Franklin et al, 2001).

We asked the students in further education about their pattern of attendance:

- all of the nine students with moderate learning difficulties and the seven with severe learning difficulties in further education attended college full time.

The majority of young people about whom information was provided, attended school or college on a daily basis:

- 15 of the students with moderate learning difficulties lived at home while seven were resident at their school or college
- 10 of the students with severe learning difficulties were day students while two returned home every two weeks, two were termly boarders and two were on 52 week placements.

All of the young people who were not day students attended general special needs or specialist schools and colleges designated for blind and partially sighted students, which offered 24 hour education and care for young people with the most profound difficulties.

12.2 Courses and qualifications

Only those students in further education or their parents were asked about the duration of their courses and of the 15 students for whom information was given:

- three were on one year courses
- seven were on two year courses
- five were on three year courses.

Between them, the students were studying a diverse range of subjects. While some parents and young people identified subjects which were related to the students' visual and learning difficulties, including mobility, general living skills, independence skills and "how to cook and eat", others said they were following vocational courses which included woodwork, belt-making and gardening. Some students were on courses concerned with basic skills such as numeracy and literacy and one student specified a range of GCSE subjects including English, mathematics and childcare.

Seventeen students said that they expected to gain qualifications at the end of their studies:

- eight students were hoping to gain vocational qualifications
- four students were studying for other qualifications including foundation courses and an assessment certificate
- four students, who said they were studying for a qualification, were unsure exactly what this qualification was called
- one student was studying for GCSEs.

12.3 Previous education

- Over half of the students for whom information was available had been in the same type of provision throughout their education.

Among the 17 students for whom this information was provided, we discovered that over half had remained in the same type of provision throughout their education:

- more than one in two of the 17 students had remained in the same type of provision, namely general specialist provision (seven students), specialist provision for blind and partially sighted students (six) and mainstream provision (four)
- of those who had moved to different types of provision, the largest number had moved from mainstream provision to other settings. Six students had moved from mainstream to general special needs provision, while two had moved to specialist provision for blind and partially sighted students
- of the remaining students who provided information on this subject, four had moved from general special needs to specialist provision for blind and partially sighted students while three, who had previously attended specialist establishments for blind and partially sighted students were now in general special needs provision.

12.4 Choice of educational placement

- Fewer than half of the parents felt they had been offered a choice of educational placement for their child.

We appreciated that the choice of educational placements for young people with learning difficulties would be influenced by a range of factors. These would include their individual needs, the kind of course they wanted to study, possibly the type of provision they had attended previously, the range of options available to them and other factors they considered to be important.

To establish the extent to which the students' educational placements reflected parental preference, we asked parents about their choice of school or college for their son or daughter. Fewer than half of the 34 parents who completed questionnaires were sure that they had been given a choice.

While 15 parents stated that they had not had a choice, 14 said they had been given a choice and five were not sure.

12.5 Factors in choosing schools and colleges

- Parents ranked support for students with sight difficulties as one of the key factors in selecting a school or college.

Table 12.1 **Choice of education placement: factors parents considered important for students with visual impairments and additional learning difficulties**

Factors in choosing a school or college	Number of parents placing factor among three most important (n=28)	Number of parents identifying factor as single most important (n=28)
The reputation of the school or college	17	6
Support for sight difficulties	14	7
Support for health needs	11	3
Near to family home	11	6
Links with the community and/or other schools	8	3
Therapies available	6	1
Equipment available	6	1
Availability of residential places	5	-
Size and layout of the school site	4	-
A wide choice of clubs and activities	1	-
Other siblings at the school	1	1

We asked parents what they considered to be the three most important factors and, of these, what they believed to be the single most important factor in selecting a school or college. The same list of options was used throughout the study, based on information gained from focus groups. It does not follow that the range of factors parents regarded as important were necessarily present in the establishments their sons or daughters attended. As highlighted previously, fewer than half of these parents felt that they had had a real choice of placement.

In selecting a school or college, parents identified a range of factors as among the three most important:

- around one in two of the parents who responded to the question placed the reputation of the school or college (17) or support for students with sight difficulties (14) among the three most important factors
- slightly fewer than one in two parents regarded the presence of support for health needs (11) and the fact that a school or college was near to their home (11) as among the three most important factors
- fewer than one in four parents considered links with the community and with other schools or colleges (eight), the availability of therapies (six), equipment (six) residential placements (five) or size and layout of the school or college (four) as among the three key factors influencing selection
- only one parent considered the availability of a wide range of clubs and activities as among the three most important factors. One other parent said the presence of siblings at the school or college was important, a factor not included in the original list provided.

When we asked which of these factors they would rank as the single most important factor in selecting a school or college for their child, the largest number of parents cited support for students with sight difficulties (seven), the reputation of the school (six) and its proximity to the family home (six). Fewer parents regarded support for health needs (three) and links with the community and with other schools or colleges (three) as the single most important factor while the availability of therapies, equipment and the presence of other siblings at the school were each mentioned only once.

Parents of young people with moderate learning difficulties and with severe learning difficulties had similar priorities when selecting a school or college. Obviously, the factors which any parent regarded as important would depend upon individual needs; for example, only the parents of students who required therapies would regard therapy as a key factor.

References

Franklin, A, Keil, S, Crofts, K and Cole-Hamilton, I (2001). **The educational experiences of 5 to 16 year-old blind and partially sighted children and young people.** Shaping the Future Report 2. Royal National Institute for the Blind, London.

Croft K, Clery L, Keil S, Franklin A and Cole-Hamilton, I (2001). **The health and wellbeing of partially sighted children and young people aged 5 to 25.** Shaping the Future Report 5. Royal National Institute for the Blind, London.

CHAPTER THIRTEEN Students' experiences at school and college

When exploring the students' experiences in post-16 education, we focused our questions on specific aspects. We asked the young people with moderate learning difficulties about the reading materials and careers advice they had received at school or college and about their experiences of using the library. Focus group discussions indicated that while these aspects of education were relevant to this group of students, they were outside the experience of most, if not all, students with complex learning difficulties. We asked the parents of young people with severe learning difficulties about the availability of equipment, therapies and support staff at school or college. In addition, we asked both groups about any difficulties the students may have encountered at school or college.

13.1 Experiences when starting at the current school or college

To begin with, we asked all the parents about their son or daughter's experiences when they started at school or college, by requesting their views on a number of statements.

Parents' responses revealed a high level of satisfaction with the students' educational placements. No more than six out of a total of 34 parents disagreed with any of the positive statements about the students' experiences at school or college. The fact that some parents were "unsure" about certain experiences stems from the fact that most would have had very limited opportunities to observe students in the educational setting and that the young people's learning difficulties might prevent them from telling their parents about every issue. For instance, six of the 31 parents who responded to the statement were unsure whether the staff at school or college understood their child's needs; it is indeed unlikely that parents would have met or observed all members of staff interacting with the young person.

Table 13.1 **Parents' comments on students' experiences when starting at their current school or college: students with moderate learning difficulties (MLD) and students with severe learning difficulties (SLD)**

Statement	Agree	Disagree	Not sure
S/he adapted easily to the new routine (n=31)	21	4	6
There were plenty of staff available (n=32)	26	2	4
S/he was able to access all parts of the school or college (n=20)	11	3	6
Transport to and from school or college was no problem (n=30)	27	2	1
The equipment s/he needs was there at the start (n=31)	21	3	7
The school or college has helped give my son/daughter confidence (n=32)	29	2	1
At school or college, s/he is learning daily living skills (n=30)	27	2	1
S/he has a wide choice of activities at school or college (n=32)	26	3	3
S/he is very happy at school or college (n=32)	28	1	3
The staff at school or college understand his/her needs (n=31)	23	6	2

n=34

13.2 Students with moderate learning difficulties

13.2.1 Support and inclusion

- The majority of students said they received the support they needed.
- A significant minority felt left out of some activities.

We provided the students with moderate learning difficulties with a range of positive and negative statements about their experiences at their current schools and colleges and asked them to say whether they agreed, disagreed or were unsure about each one. This was a very small sample of 17, but the responses indicate that, while these students generally felt that they were getting the help they needed and had someone to talk to if there was a problem at school or college, significant numbers felt that they were left out of classroom and social activities because of their sight difficulties:

- 15 students stated that they were getting the help they needed at school or college, one student said they were not, and one was unsure
- 15 students said that if there was a problem at school or college, they usually had someone to talk to; one student said they did not and one student was unsure
- six of the 17 students said that they sometimes got left out of classroom activities because of their sight difficulties; five said that they were not left out and the remaining six did not respond
- while six students said that they sometimes got left out of social activities as a result of their sight difficulties, nine stated that this did not happen and two students were unsure about this.

All of the students who experienced problems with support and sometimes being left out were either in general specialist or mainstream provision. None attended specialist provision for blind and partially sighted students:

- the two students who said they did not get the help they needed at school and did not usually have someone to talk to when there was a problem were both in general provision for special needs
- all six of the students who felt that they were sometimes left out of classroom activities because of their sight difficulties were in general special needs provision

- while four of the students who said they were sometimes left out of social activities as a result of their sight difficulties were in general special needs provision, the remaining two students who felt this way were both in mainstream placements.

Although these numbers are too small to allow us to draw general conclusions, they support the hypothesis that blind and partially sighted students in mainstream or general special needs provision are more likely to feel excluded from some classroom or social activities because of their sight difficulties than those in specialist provision for blind and partially sighted students.

13.2.2 Reading materials

- Most students received reading materials in their preferred format.

We asked the students with moderate learning difficulties about their preferred reading medium. It emerged that many of the students liked to use a combination of media, of which the most popular were large print and tape. While 12 students used large print and nine used tape, four used standard print, three liked computer disks and one used braille. When we asked the students to identify their favourite reading medium, ten students cited large print, three said standard print, two identified tape, and one student expressed an equal preference for braille or disk.

Almost all of the students (15 of the 17) were given their preferred media for the reading materials they used at school or college. The two exceptions were one student who preferred tape but received and used braille and another who preferred large print but received standard print. As these observations relate only to this small group of 17 students, no general conclusions can be drawn.

13.2.3 Using school and college libraries

We put our questions about library use to the 17 students with moderate learning difficulties who completed the questionnaire themselves, as we knew that students in this group would be the most likely to use these facilities. All of these students told us whether they had found using the library in their current school or college "easy", "OK", or "difficult" or said that they had not used this facility.

While seven students found using the library "easy", one stated that this was "OK" while four had found this to be "difficult" and the remaining five students said they had not used the facility. Some students explained that they did not think they needed to use the library; for example these included one student at a specialist FE college who was taking music, literacy, numeracy and fitness and another taking an NVQ in gardening in a mainstream FE college.

We discovered elsewhere in this survey that using libraries posed a problem for many of the young people of around average learning ability who were blind or partially sighted. Many of these students said their difficulties with library use were finding materials and the fact that materials were rarely in their preferred medium. Similar problems were identified by some of the students with moderate learning difficulties who found using the library difficult, for example:

"It is hard to find the right books, knowing where they are, and seeing where they are. "

Student at mainstream FE college

"No help or time [available]."

Student at mainstream FE college

"The computers and print are standard and the print is not enlarged enough."

Student at FE college

A number of the students had additional physical disabilities which could present problems in using the library, as individual students discovered:

"Because I use a wheelchair it's difficult to find someone to take me."

FE college student

"Because the library is not accessible. It has stairs that are hard to get around."

Student at mainstream sixth form college

To enable these students with moderate learning difficulties to use the libraries in their schools and colleges, providers clearly need to address access issues relating to visual impairment and to the physical environment.

13.2.4 **Careers advice**

- The majority of students had received careers advice.

As with library use, we appreciated that questions concerned with careers advice would be most relevant to those students for whom future employment was a viable option. We therefore asked the students with moderate learning difficulties who completed questionnaires for themselves whether they had received any advice about what to do when they left college, who had given the advice and how useful it had been. This question was not put to students with severe, complex learning difficulties or their parents.

Fourteen of the 17 students with moderate learning difficulties stated that they had received careers advice and the three who had not received this all said that they would like the opportunity to talk to someone about their future. Between them, the 14 students had received careers advice from 19 individuals. In most cases, these were careers advisers:

- six students had received advice from special needs careers advisers
- six students had talked to general careers advisers
- four of the students had received advice from teachers or lecturers
- two of the students had received careers advice from a social worker
- one student had spoken to an RNIB student adviser.

Twelve of the 14 students who had received careers advice commented upon the quality of this advice. While seven stated that the advice had been helpful, two claimed that this was not the case and three were unsure how helpful the advice had been.

13.3 **Students with severe learning difficulties**

When examining the educational experiences of the students with complex needs and severe learning difficulties, we wanted to find out not only whether the specialist equipment, therapists and support staff which they required were available, but also whether their complex difficulties presented problems at school or college. Parents in focus groups had identified a range of problems experienced by blind and partially sighted students with severe learning difficulties. These issues were used to prepare a list of statements. About half of the parents who responded to a range of statements about the experiences of their children at school or college indicated that their complex difficulties did cause problems:

- five of the 19 parents who responded to the question claimed that the student was disrupted by other students who were noisy in class
- four parents felt that the other students' needs were different from those of their son or daughter
- two parents said that the student missed a lot of college or school because of health difficulties
- just one parent said that the teachers did not understand the sensory needs of their child
- nine of the 19 parents who responded to these questions indicated that they had no concerns about any of these issues.

13.3.1 Availability of equipment, therapists and support staff

- The majority of parents said that the resources needed were usually available.

We asked parents whether they believed that the specialist equipment, therapies and support staff their children required were "always", "sometimes" or "never" available. As shown in table 13.1, most parents said that the resources required were usually available. The significant numbers of parents who were "unsure" whether therapists, support staff and various pieces of equipment were available at school or college is likely to result from the fact that they had limited opportunities to observe their son or daughter in this setting.

Table 13.1 **Parents' views on availability of specialist resources at school or college**

Resource	Always	Some-times	Never available	Not sure
Soft play area (n=11)	8	2	-	1
Closed circuit television (n=9)	2	1	1	5
Computer (n=13)	7	4	-	2
Switches for communication (n=11)	3	3	-	5
Sensory stimulation room (n=10)	5	4	-	1
Specially adapted toilet (n=10)	8	1	-	1
Magnifier or low vision aid (n=8)	1	-	2	5
Tape recorder (n=14)	9	3	-	2
Physiotherapist (n=12)	3	7	2	-
Speech and language therapist (n=14)	3	10	1	-
Occupational therapist (n=11)	2	4	1	4
One to one classroom assistant (n=17)	4	13	-	-
Interpreter (n=4)	3	1	-	-
Specialist teacher (n=15)	12	1	1	1
Play therapist (n=9)	2	-	3	4
Reflexologist (n=11)	2	4	4	1
Music therapist (n=13)	3	5	2	3
Doctor (n=12)	6	6	-	-
Nurse (n=11)	6	5	-	-
Mobility instructor (n=10)	3	4	-	3

13.4 **Bullying**

- Almost half of the students said they had been bullied to some degree.

We asked both the students with moderate learning difficulties and the parents of young people with more complex difficulties a series of questions about bullying, as both groups might experience this. Only about one respondent in four believed that bullying took place in the student's school or college but almost one in two of the students themselves said they had been bullied to some degree. These findings are not contradictory as a number of students were bullied outside their current school or college:

- of the 40 individuals who responded to the question, ten respondents stated that bullying did happen in the student's school or college while 21 stated that it did not and nine others were unsure
- while 15 respondents said that the student had been bullied a lot and four claimed that they had been bullied a little, 18 respondents stated that the student had not experienced any bullying, while five respondents were unsure.

Unsurprisingly, the nine respondents who were unsure about bullying were all parents. Logically, parents would be less likely than their children to know about bullying at school or college.

When we asked the students and parents who had been involved in the bullying, it emerged that other students at the young person's school or college mainly perpetrated this:

- 13 respondents indicated that the student had been bullied by other students at school or college. Five young people said they had been bullied by other students of their own age outside school and three said they had been bullied by their teachers.

Seventeen responses provided details of the bullying behaviour, the most common forms of which were name-calling and violent behaviour. Some students had experienced more than one form of bullying:

- ten students said that they had been called names
- six students had experienced violence which included pushing and hitting and one having their hair singed

- three students said they had been threatened
- two students said things had been thrown at them
- other incidents which the students defined as "bullying" included having their belongings taken, being left out of activities and generally being ignored.

About half of the students who had been bullied (10 out of 19) had found someone to talk to about the incidents which had taken place.

CHAPTER FOURTEEN What would improve schools and colleges?

Having investigated the different areas of school and college life for the students with learning difficulties, we asked the 34 parents who had completed questionnaires how satisfied they were overall with their child's current education and what would improve it. The 32 parents who responded to this question demonstrated a high level of satisfaction. Twenty five parents stated that they were satisfied with their son or daughter's school or college while just two parents claimed to be unsatisfied and four others said they were not sure about this issue.

A number of parents commented on the reasons for their satisfaction or dissatisfaction with their child's current educational placement. While it is important to remember that we are dealing with a small sample of 34 parents, a range of issues emerged as important to a number of these parents, many of which echoed the views of other parents and students in the study.

14.1 Access to information

Several parents voiced their concerns about the accessibility of information provided at school or college, an issue also raised by a number of the students of around average learning ability. Parents suggested the following changes that would improve students' access to the curriculum:

"Large print on paperwork and books."

"Large print books which he can understand."

"Tapes with slower speech so he understands it."

14.2 Involvement in the local community

A number of parents appeared concerned that the young people's social experiences were limited to their school or college, giving few opportunities for them to become involved in the local community. While one parent said that "the whole social setting seems to revolve around college without much outside contact," others stated that the young people's lives would improve with:

"More outside activities."

"(The) ability to get off campus to social activities."

"More involvement in the community."

"More structured out of college experiences."

14.3 Proximity of schools and colleges to home

The distances students travelled to their educational placements, which many parents identified as the most important factor in the selection of a school or college, also appeared to influence their satisfaction with the schools and colleges. While one parent was satisfied with the placement because, "it is fairly near home", another complained that her child's education placement was 450 miles from home. These concerns were similar to those expressed by some of the parents of children and young people of around average learning ability in the survey who had also to travel significant distances to access specialist provision.

14.4 Staff expertise

A number of parents who were dissatisfied with some aspects of the student's placement felt that life would be improved if staff had a greater understanding of individual needs. In particular, some parents seemed concerned that schools and colleges had expertise in meeting some, but not all, of the young people's needs:

"As our daughter adapts quickly, it has been difficult to convince staff that there is a visual problem. Literature about nystagmus would enable staff to understand the situation."

Parent of a mainstream school student

"X needs a school for speech and language difficulties as well as sight and the only school that can help him is a boarding school which we do not want."

Parent of a student in a specialist school

"More time spent on daily living skills."

Parent of a student at specialist FE college

Other parents who were satisfied with their children's educational placements described how these had enabled the young person to develop in a number of areas:

"X has matured and made progress towards independence and made many friends. He has learned work skills which will enable him to make a contribution to society when he leaves."

Parent of a student at a specialist FE college for blind and partially sighted students

"Within the school he has become more confident and able."

Parent of a student at specialist FE college

"He has settled in well and already won a trophy for achievement."

Parent of a student at college, placement details not given

"She is happy, has friends and does lots of activities."

Parent of a student in mainstream FE college

Clearly, the nature and quality of the educational placements of the young people with learning difficulties aged between 16 and 25 varied significantly. However, it is notable that, although the difficulties and needs of this group differed substantially from those of the young people of around average learning ability and the younger children with additional complex needs, many of the areas for improvement which they and their parents identified were similar to those described elsewhere.

APPENDIX Education Authorities and Boards, colleges and universities taking part in the research

Blind and partially sighted children and young people from schools and further education colleges in the following Education Authorities and Boards took part in the research:

EDUCATION AUTHORITIES
England

Barnsley
Bath and North East Somerset
Bedfordshire
Birmingham
Bromley
Buckinghamshire
Cornwall
Coventry
Doncaster
Dudley
East Sussex
Essex
Gloucestershire
Hampshire
Havering
Herefordshire
Hertfordshire
Hounslow
Kent
Kirklees
Lambeth
Lancashire
Leeds
Leicestershire
Liverpool

Manchester
Milton Keynes
Newcastle
Newham
Northamptonshire
North Yorkshire
Northumberland
Nottinghamshire
Oldham
Redbridge
Salford
Sheffield
Shropshire
Somerset
South Tyneside
Staffordshire
Stockport
Suffolk
Surrey
Wandsworth
Westminster
Worcestershire
Wirral

Wales
Cardiff
Carmarthenshire
Flintshire
Gwynedd and Anglesey
Neath
Newport/Caerphilly
Rhondda
Swansea

Scotland
Dumfries and Galloway
Edinburgh
Falkirk
Fife
Glasgow
North Lanarkshire
Orkney
South Lanarkshire

Education Boards
Northern Ireland
Belfast
Southern
Western

Students from the following universities and colleges of higher education took part in the research

England
University of East Anglia
University of Greenwich
Liverpool John Moore's University
Leeds Metropolitan University
University of Manchester
Nene College of Higher Education
The Nottingham Trent University
University of Reading
Sheffield Hallam University
Staffordshire University
University of Sunderland
University of Surrey
University of Warwick

Wales
University of Wales, Cardiff
Swansea Institute of Higher Education

Scotland
University of Abertay, Dundee
University of Strathclyde